Gnomes

"To my amazement I have heard that there are people who have never seen a gnome. I can't help pitying these people. I am certain there must be something wrong with their eyesight."

Axel Munthe

text by
Wil Huygen

illustrated by
Rien Poortvliet

Originally published under the title *leven en werken de Kabouter*
© 1976 Unieboek B. V./Van Holkema & Warendorf, Bussum, The Netherlands
English translation copyright © 1977 Unieboek B.V./Van Holkema & Warendorf

Library of Congress Catalog Card Number: 77-82805;
Peacock Press/Bantam Books Edition: SBN 01131-6
Printed and bound in the United States of America

Gnomes

HARRY N. ABRAMS, INC., PUBLISHERS, NEW YORK

PEACOCK PRESS/BANTAM BOOKS • TORONTO NEW YORK LONDON

Introduction

Now, after twenty years of observation, we feel that the time has come to put our experiences and findings on paper, having received permission, of course, from an authorized council of gnomes—which, by the way, took all of five years to make its decision. It is our belief that this book fills a deplorable gap, for the published literature on gnomes is virtually nonexistent. One of the chief sources of information has been Wilhelm J. Wunderlich's bulky treatise *De Hominibus Parvissimis (Concerning the Wee People)* published in 1580. It contains a number of striking details, but, alas, confuses gnomes with dwarfs and dubious fairy tale characters so often that its overall reliability is negligible.

Today, gnomes are nearly forgotten beings. Since they work by night in the woods and sometimes in human dwellings, it is not sheer coincidence that the word gnome itself is derived from *Kuba-Walda,* which means "home administrator" or "home spirit" in the ancient Germanic language. In rural areas these home administrators often live in the rafters of barns, where, if they are treated well,

they keep an eye on the livestock as well as crops. Another variant of their name translates as "to put in order" or "to do odd jobs"—with or without an apron.

In earlier times the gnome was an accepted member of society in Europe, Russia, and Siberia. Gnomes were seen regularly and people in all stations of life were rewarded or punished, helped or hindered by them (depending on their own attitudes)—a situation they came to find quite normal. But that was a time when waters were clear and forests virginal, when roads led peacefully from one settlement to another, when the heavens were filled only with birds and stars.

Since that time, gnomes have been forced to retreat into hidden corners above and below the ground, where they keep well out of sight, so much so in fact that belief in their existence is waning rapidly. Nevertheless, just as if you do not look carefully you will fail to see a hare in a meadow or a deer in a forest, so it is with gnomes: you may not see them, but they are there, all right!

Now that we are so concerned with saving what is left of nature's treasures, there is some hope that gnomes will begin to move about more freely. More and more people are beginning to realize that they have a neglected

but forgiving and wise mother in Nature. These people will undoubtedly meet gnomes. We dedicate this book to them in the hope that they will gain much pleasure from their encounters.

The gnomes consulted for this book were extremely reserved when pressed for answers to some of our questions, and as a result there are certain deficiencies or imperfections in our work. Valuable supplementary data from well-informed readers will therefore be most welcome. It will be included (with sources mentioned) in subsequent editions.

Although the woodland gnome is treated in greatest detail in this volume, other types are also dealt with. Gnomes, of course, are twilight and night creatures, and because of this we had to conduct our investigations in near or total darkness. Had we been completely true to our observations, many illustrations in this book would have been painted in blue or dull gray. To overcome this difficulty and provide an accurate picture of gnome life, the illustrations are colored as if the subjects had been observed in broad daylight.

een poortoliet
Wil Huygen

Historical Background

Round about A.D. 1200, the Swede Frederik Ugarph found a well-preserved wooden statue in a fisherman's house in Nidaros (now Trondheim) in Norway. The statue was 15 cm. (just under 6 in.) high, not including the pedestal. Engraved on the pedestal were the words:

NISSE
Riktig Størrelse

which means "Gnome, actual height."

The statue had been in the fisherman's family as long as anyone could remember, and Ugarph succeeded in buying it only after days of negotiation. It is now part of the Oliv family collection in Uppsala. X-ray tests have proved the statue to be more than 2,000 years old. It must have been carved from the roots of a tree that is no longer known; the wood is incredibly hard. The letters were carved many centuries later. The statue's discovery and dating illustrate what gnomes themselves have always said—that their origins are early Scandinavian.

It was only after the Great People's Migration beginning A.D. 395 that gnomes appear in the Low Lands—probably in 449, when the Roman outpost of Britannia fell to the Anglo-Saxons and Jutes. Some evidence of this comes from the statement of a pensioned Roman sergeant, Publius Octavus, who owned a villa and farm in the woods outside Lugdunum (now Leiden, in Holland). He had married a local woman and so did not return to Rome. It was pure luck that his property was spared destruction at the hands of the barbarians.

Publius Octavus wrote the following description in A.D. 470:

"Today I saw a miniature person with my own eyes. He wore a red cap and blue shirt. He had a white beard and green pants. He said that he had lived in this land for twenty years. He spoke our language, mixed with strange

the statue in Uppsala

words. Since then I have spoken with the little man many times. He said he was a descendant of a race called Kuwalden, a word unknown to us, and that there were only a few of them in the world. He liked to drink milk. Time and again I saw him cure sick animals in the meadows."

In the chaotic times up until 500, after Odoacer, king of the Germans, had disposed of the last ruler of the Western Roman Empire, the gnomes must have established themselves in Europe, Russia, and Siberia, although exact information is lacking. Actually, gnomes find writing history uninteresting, or at least pretend to, but it is rumored that they have certain secret records.

In his book of 1580, Wunderlich mentions that in his time gnomes had maintained a classless society for more than 1,000 years. Except for their own chosen king, there were no rich, poor, inferior, or superior gnomes. This is perhaps why they made use of the Great People's Migration to begin afresh. It all sounds plausible until he tells of a map (now lost) of a gnome king's palace and adjacent gold mines; apparently slave labor was used in the mines, and sometimes there were slave revolts.

Using our scant information as a guide, we must conclude that gnomes gradually sought more contact with the people they lived among, and that they were completely integrated into our society 50 to 100 years before the reign of Charlemagne (768–814).

The adult male gnome weighs
300 grams

The adult female gnome weighs →
250 - 275
grams

Geographical Range

Dispersion in North America

The map above shows a number of sites in North America where gnomes are reported to exist. The difficulty with establishing to a certainty that gnomes do indeed live on the continent has been that no sighting or encounter can be confirmed unless witnessed by two observers—the same criteria are used by bird watchers. Thus, though considerable evidence has accumulated, none of it is reported in this book. It can be surmised, however, that American gnomes (whose geographical range corresponds to their fellows' climate and life zones in Europe) do adopt the same dress, life styles, and behavior patterns as their cousins across the sea.

Dispersion in Europe

Western Border: Irish Coast.
Eastern Border: Deep in Siberia.
Northern Border: Norway, Sweden, Finland, Russia, and Siberia.
Southern Border: In a line from the Belgian coast via Switzerland, the Balkans, Upper Black Sea, Caucasus, Siberia. (This has to do with the shorter days and longer winter nights occurring in the lands north of the line.)

Names for Gnomes in Various Languages

Irish	Gnome	Polish	Gnom
English	Gnome	Finnish	Tonttu
Flemish	Kleinmanneken	Russian	Domovoi Djèdoesjka
Dutch	Kabouter	Serbo-Croatian	Kippec; Patuljak
German	Heinzelmännchen	Bulgarian	Djudjè
Norwegian	Tomte or Nisse	Czechoslovakian	Skritek
Swedish	Tomtebisse or Nisse	Hungarian	Manó
Danish	Nisse		

WOODLAND GNOME

275 years old

in the prime of life

actual height (without cap)

15 cm.

his frowning is due to posing in harsh daylight...

Tool kit attached to belt

Feet slightly turned inward to insure great speed (over grass, etc...)

Daily dress —
Camouflage colors

ELDERLY FEMALE GNOME 346 years
(when 350 years or older she begins to show a light beard)

Physical Appearance

There are male and female gnomes. In our daily lives, we come in contact only with the male, because the female almost always stays at home.

THE MALE wears a peaked red cap. He has a full beard which becomes gray long before his hair does.

He wears a blue smock *) with a Byronic collar or caftan neck (usually covered up by his beard).

Around his waist he wears a leather belt with tool kit attached, consisting of knife, hammer, drill, files, etc.

Next, the brown-green pants and footwear

felt boots

shoes of birch bark

or wooden clogs

depending on the area in which he lives.

*) The droll riddling rhyme from the opera *Hänsel und Gretel*—

Ein Männlein steht im Walde ganz still und stumm;
Es hat von lauter Purper ein Mäntlein um.
Sagt, wer mag das Männlein sein, . . . das da steht auf einem
  Bein. . . .

(A little man stands in the woods, still and alone;
His smock is of bright purple and with purple thread is
  sewn.
Pray tell: who is this little man, . . . who stands upon
  just one leg. . . .)

—has nothing to do with gnomes; it concerns a toadstool, most likely the fly fungus. The confusion probably stems from the unproven folk belief that gnomes, in times of danger, can transform themselves into toadstools.

Facial coloring is fair but with red apple cheeks, especially in old age.

The nose is straight or slightly turned up. The eyes are generally gray; the few variations are due to cross-breeding with Trolls in primeval times.

The eyes are surrounded by many wrinkles mainly

laugh wrinkles

which doesn't alter the fact that they can all of a sudden look penetratingly serious. Gnomes do not so much see the material presence of those before them; rather, they probe the real self and view the landscape therein to such an extent that no secrets remain.

Greetings, farewells and goodnights

are expressed by rubbing noses.

It is said that this allows for a more penetrating glance into the eyes. Hardly likely. It is probably nothing more than just a friendly gesture and, anyway, gnomes have no secrets from one another. In fact, they have only to glance at someone in the distance and right away they know what is happening in that person's inner self.

The gnome's conspicuous dress serves to
protect him from birds of prey during
the twilight and night hours. They are his
friends but could mistake a fast-moving gnome for a large mouse
were it not for his red cap.

Which only goes to prove that birds _can_ see colors, a fact
biologists doubt, even today.

On the other hand, his bright
clothing could be a disadvantage
when the gnome meets the more
annoying creatures of his life, such
as martens, cats, snakes,
Polecats, ermine, and hornets!

A night-hunting owl

Still, the gnome doesn't fret too much about these bothersome creatures, as he far surpasses them in intelligence.

The gnome moves at such tearing speed—when he wants to—even on long journeys, that he could easily outdistance most predatory creatures, with the exception, perhaps, of the hornet. The hornet, however, stings only during the daylight hours, and the gnome is usually indoors then. When a gnome has a daytime mission to carry out, he first rubs himself all over with the juice of the nux vomica, or vomit nut, plant; a small quantity of this noxious material causes a tendency to vomit in all who inhale it (save the gnome himself) and thereby discourages the sting-eager hornet.

FOOTPRINTS

The footprints left behind by a gnome are very distinctive—if you can find them! In order not to leave a trail as he walks along, a gnome makes clever use of pebbles, hard pieces of moss, and pine needles; by stepping on them rather than on the bare ground he leaves no tracks. Sometimes he walks in a circle or back upon his own trail, or proceeds through the trees. If he knows for certain that he is being followed, he will almost always disappear into an underground passage.

When forced to tread on bare ground, the gnome makes use of a bird's-foot pattern printed in relief on the soles of his boots. With this cunning aid he disguises his travels. But gnomes sometimes give themselves away by betraying the following small vanity: if you come across a birch leaf on the ground with a clear blob of slime in its middle, you can be sure that a gnome has just passed by and exercised his skill in target spitting. He can't resist proving his aim—and thus leaves a trail.

The clothing mentioned is worn summer and winter without an overcoat, for the male gnome adjusts well to all kinds of weather. At the most he may wear an extra **vest** or **long johns** during extreme cold.

THE FEMALE

Wears gray or khaki clothing

Until she is married she wears a green cap, with her braids sticking out

girl of 96 years (still shy!) →

After marriage, her hair disappears under a scarf and darker cap.

woman 316 years

← although the female gnome has a substantial bosom, decreased gravity (at her height) allows her to go through life unencumbered by a brassiere!

blouse

skirt to ankles

black-gray knee socks

and high shoes or slippers

Mainly because of the gray color of her clothing, the female gnome feels safer indoors; mistaking females for small forest animals, owls could very easily cause deep wounds with their talons before realizing that they had attacked a friend. An advantage of the clothing is that humans have difficulty spotting female gnomes because their dress blends with the background so well. When a female gnome is picked up, she often disarms her captor by playing possum until she is released.

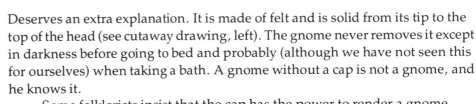

Deserves an extra explanation. It is made of felt and is solid from its tip to the top of the head (see cutaway drawing, left). The gnome never removes it except in darkness before going to bed and probably (although we have not seen this for ourselves) when taking a bath. A gnome without a cap is not a gnome, and he knows it.

Some folklorists insist that the cap has the power to render a gnome invisible, but if this is so, it is not its principal function. Rather, it is an indispensable head covering, protection against such unsuspected blows from above as are dealt by falling twigs, acorns, or hailstones, and against attacks by animals of prey. (Interestingly, just as a lizard will surrender its tail in order to escape, so the gnome will give up his cap to a marauding cat.)

The gnome reveals his individuality as much with his cap as with the shape of his nose. A gnome child receives a cap at a very tender age and keeps it throughout life. Because it is seldom removed, wear and tear on the cap is considerable, and with great care new layers of felt are periodically added to the outside. This work is done every few years with the help of a form molded in the exact shape of the gnome's head.

cross
section

↓

Gnome working at the **Cap form**
a job that he hates!!

It is tedious work. But he would rather be
without his pants than without his cap.
(Notice that he covers his bare head with a cloth
while uncapped.)

Physiology

Skeleton
Muscular system
Circulatory system
Brain and nerve center
Digestive system
Kidney and bladder system
Respiratory system
Connective tissue
Skin + hair
Blood
Senses
Hormonal system
Sexual organs

↖ The brainpan is relatively larger than that of humans.
8 pairs of ribs, 4 floating ribs (humans, 7 and 5)
arms longer, legs shorter, foot bones and arch extra powerful.

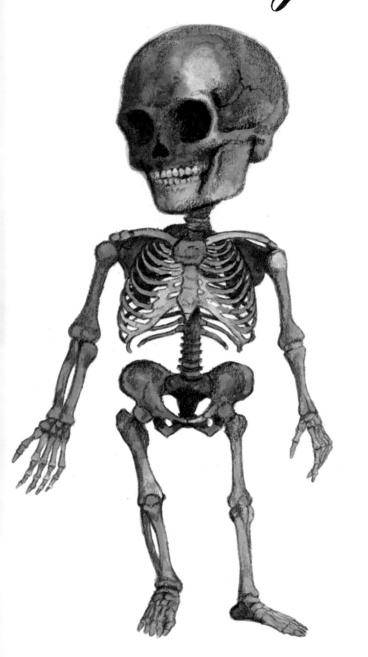

Skeleton

Nature seems to find it necessary to produce two sizes in many of her creations: horse, pony; stag, hind; rat, mouse; hare, rabbit; and goose, duck. And so we have human and gnome; however, the difference in size is so extreme that the similarity is all the more striking. Following is a description of the (slight) differences in physical makeup between man and gnome:

Goose

Duck

Muscular System

Because—going from large to small—the volume, and therefore the weight, of an object decreases as the cube of its linear dimension and the surface area only as the square, even a fat gnome moves more easily than a man (compare a flea to an elephant). Gnomes can therefore run much faster, can jump higher, and are seven times stronger than man, relatively speaking.

Gnome leg muscles have an extra muscle bundle. Further, the gnome has two types of muscles—red and white. The white are for short-distance performance; they permit the accumulation of extra oxygen, which is later discharged through panting breaths. The red muscles are responsible for endurance work.

Man has rudimentary ear muscles; these are more powerfully developed in the gnome, so he can point his ears in any direction.

Gnome with ears pricked up →

7 times as strong as a man . . .

Circulatory System

Heart relatively large (athlete, race-horse).

Blood vessels, wide and of good quality (heart attacks are unknown).

More blood circulation than in man (adjustment to cold, power of endurance).

Hardening of the arteries known only after 400th year.

Brain and Nerve Center

Brain capacity larger than man's.

Digestive System

Total length of the intestines greater than man's (gnomes do not eat meat). Liver more robust, gall bladder smaller. Gallstones unknown.

Kidney and Bladder System

Urine can be contained for a whole day.

Respiratory System

Lungs relatively large and deep (power of endurance, high running speeds).

Connective Tissue, Skin, and Hair

Connective tissue extremely stiff and tough. Hair becomes gray very early. Baldness unknown.

Senses

EYE
Cornea, lens, iris, retina (containing rods and cones).

Yellow spot contains 8 million cones; man has only a few and therefore has limited vision in the dark. The gnome, however, also has a high concentration of bars in the yellow spot, like the owl; this allows for sharp vision in the dark. Further, the very flexible pupil allows for maximum light intake.

EAR
External auditory canal short and wide.

Auricle relatively large and can be pointed in any direction and revolved.

Not tone-deaf.

Transmission to the brain occurs with greater electrical capacity.

SMELL
Mucous membrane to be found in *all* nose cavities, which explains the great nose size. Radio-light

connection by transmission of smell to brain (dog and fox).

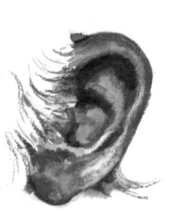

TASTE
As with humans, only four qualities are perceptible: sweet, sour, salt, bitter (the rest is "tasted" by the mucous membrane in nose).

TOUCH
Fingertips as sensitive as those of a blind person. Fingerprints are mainly of a circular pattern.

The World of Smell

Like animals, the gnome "sees" a great deal of the world through his nose. Even if he should become blind and deaf he would still be able to recognize his whereabouts and know what was happening about him in the forest: a familiar smell guides his every step.

Man no longer has this gift, though echoes of it still return in a spring breeze, the perfume of flowers, the scent of old farm villages, or a sudden smell of the sea, which somehow remind us of a happy youth, or of days gone by. City people use their noses only to take note of cruder smells such as smoke, perfume, food, kitchen smells, body odors.

The nose, however, is also good for "tasting" flavors. Except for sweet, sour, salt, and bitter—which are tasted by the tongue papillae—other oral flavors are transported, via the mucous membrane of the nose, through the throat and nose cavities for further discrimination (see PHYSIOLOGY: *Taste*).

For most animals (including fish and insects) the nose is just as important as the eyes and ears—if not more so. Gnomes' fine noses are used to seek out food (hyena up to 10 km.) and judge its value (the dog has an extra "nose" behind his teeth); for sex (butterflies up to 11 km.); for recognizing friend or enemy; for refinding their own tracks; and for orientation in unknown territory. In short, the nose provides most creatures with continuous information—information humans are obliged to do without. Our mucous membrane is no longer sufficiently powerful: it lies high in our nose cavity and covers only 5 cm.^{2}—a German Shepherd 150 cm.^{2}; a gnome 60 cm.^{2}. Or expressed in numbers of sensory smell cells:

Human: 5 million
Dachshund: 125 million
Fox Terrier: 147 million
German Shepherd: 220 million
Gnome: 95 million

The gnome, therefore, can smell 19 times better than man. Measurement with the olfactometer, however, reveals that his nose is actually 100,000 times better because of the finer quality of the sensory cells—as in the fox, deer, or dog.

Smelling something occurs when the nose inhales a number of molecules given off by a particular substance. For example, footprints have an odor caused by butyric acid. Butyric acid is a strong-smelling stuff emitted via the sole of the foot (also in armpit and on the skin). It can easily pass through a leather shoe; even after 48 hours a rubber boot is still saturated with the odor. With every step one takes, some millions of butyric acid molecules pass through the shoe sole, enough to be immediately identified by animal and gnome. Furthermore, they know if the scent is coming from left to right or vice versa. If they follow the wrong direction, within seconds they become aware that the butyric acid molecules have decreased (by evaporation) and turn back.

A good nose can register an unlimited number of smells; in fact, it can pick up the scent of anything on earth. To mention a few pertaining to the gnome: he can smell the types of trees, herbs, grasses, bushes, mosses; all creeping, flying, warm- and cold-blooded animals; stones, water, metal; and above all, of course, all activities pertaining to humans.

You are a keen observer if you can spot the doe in this landscape. But there seem to be no other signs of animals. At least to us. But for someone with a good nose there are all sorts of things to be discovered! (See next page.)

Let us "look" at this scene through the nose of a gnome on his way home at daybreak. Just as we can see this pebbly path through the woods on a fresh snowy morning, he can perceive (even in pitch dark) what has passed over and around it. Here are his observations:

Between midnight and 1:30 A.M., a badger trotted through (green dotted line).

Around 3:00, a mother fox took the path, leaving it here and there to sniff around (red dotted line).

About 4:00, a second fox appeared—a young male out courting (curving red dotted line).

At 4:30 a wild boar returned from grazing (blue dotted line).

Rabbits were hopping around all night (black dotted lines).

At about 8:15 P.M. the previous evening, two stags set out to graze (yellow dotted line)—and are probably still in the woods.

Fifteen minutes ago a doe began her morning ramble (pink dotted line).

These are the main things the gnome immediately observes. Many other details, such as the passage of two moles, the traversing of a weasel, the simple hopping of a hare, the rooting of beetles in the earth, the stepping about of pheasants, and the general activities of other small fry would certainly have caught his attention.

[As you can imagine, a cold in the nose is not funny to a gnome.]

EXTRASENSORY PERCEPTION

Nonverbal communication over great distances (fire, earthquake, flood).

Weather forecasting (thunder, storm, rain, high- and low-pressure areas); see THE GNOME AND THE WEATHER.

Sense of direction (as good as a homing pigeon, migratory bird). Compasses are not used. If a gnome receives one as a gift he generally hangs it on the living-room wall.

With the divining rod

Hormones and Sex Organs

Research in this area was difficult. In the literature everyone remains scrupulously silent on the subject. As well as ordinary adrenaline in the blood, gnomes have a type of super-adrenaline that makes for high-level performance in matters involving strength, stamina, and sexual drive. The sex organs are similar in form to those of the human. The female ovulates only once in her life. Exactly how that works, we do not know—but it probably became the norm through some magical intervention about 1,500 years ago. The male remains potent until about 350 years of age.

Illness and Remedies

Because gnomes live so long, one might presume that their blood pressure gets very high.

The gnome protects himself against this not only by using very little salt in his diet, but also by regularly drinking shepherd's Purse tea.

2 grams of fresh Shepherd's Purse tea to 50 cm³ boiling water.

Shepherd's Purse

Because the males don't spare themselves and are active in all types of weather, they do have a tendency to

rheumatic complaints

Externally, they use arnica, and, internally, tea made from dried stinging nettles

Stinging Nettle

As a protection against flu and colds and infections of the bronchial passages, they brew tea from Elder Blossoms.

for gargling
Selfheal
Prunella vulgaris

Elder Blossoms

For curing diarrhoea and other problems of the digestive system:

Poppy juice or opium extracted through a cut in a ripening poppyhead.

Poppy

Camomile or dill seed tea are used for curing insomnia.

Camomile

To prevent flatulence they drink fennel seed tea.

Fennel

A few pieces of dandelion leaf daily to help against constipation.

Dandelion

A daily leaf of centaury helps against hardening of the arteries.

Centaury Plant

To cure depression and general listlessness (doesn't happen very often) they use St. John's Wort tea or the tea drawn from the white fibers of a walnut.

St. John's-Wort

To prevent kidney stones they use a tea drawn from a young birch tree leaf.

Birch Leaf

For the rest, they are not plagued with any other illnesses of importance.

Injuries

For a Broken leg

comfrey is rubbed onto the skin, and the leg is then set with sawn-off elder twigs.

Profusely bleeding wounds

are staunched with yellow flag. Another good remedy is **Purple loosestrife**

STITCHING THE WOUND

Just as we do, gnomes use a curved needle and boiled flax thread. Needles and tweezers are boiled in oil. Poppy milk is dripped into the wound as an anæsthetic.

FOR BURNS

1st degree: Rub on oil

2nd degree: (blisters) A brew of oak or maple bark is placed on the wound. (Gnomes have known for ages that freshly ironed and folded bandages can cause no infection.)

3rd degree: no statement (never happens)

FOR BOILS:

Tincture of **RANUNCULUS** (Anemone pratensis, L.)

Sprains, Strains, Muscle pulls:

An ointment made from arnica and leaves is applied.
Further, treat as for a broken leg.

Insect bites:

Vinegar made from fermented fruits.
Apply tincture of **Ledum**

(Ledum-palustre)

Hornet stings:

Apply tourniquet, cut wound open, allow to bleed.

Snake bites:
Apply tourniquet, open wound, and suck out poison.

If this does not have the desired effect, or if one's life is still in peril, speedy transport to the gnome royal court is the next best thing. There, a Cure-all (a semi-sorcerer) has all kinds of antidotes at hand.

Transport of the Injured

If a male gnome is so badly wounded that he cannot move, he calls upon other gnomes for assistance by whistling a staccato tune taught him by his father. This special signal is used only in emergencies. Gnomes never "cry wolf"! The gnomes who hear the wounded gnome's signal rush to his aid, then transport him to his house on a stretcher made from two sticks.

If the patient's condition remains urgent, then the "transportation of emergency cases" phase is put into operation. One of the gnome orderlies rushes out in search of a hen pheasant, whistling in a special tone used only for this purpose. Meanwhile, two other gnomes weave a stretcher of fine birch twigs. Weaving time? Just 10 to 15 minutes! Two belts are attached to the head and foot of the stretcher; a third is connected to the middle (this will go around the hen pheasant's neck).

Then the fast fowl hurries at double time to one of the medicine men (half sorcerer, half doctor) at the nearest royal court. If necessary, she can fly over any body of water or danger zones in her path.

The gnome's life-span is around **400** years.

They lead healthy lives. They don't eat too much, have few emotional problems, and get plenty of excercise.

They do indulge in pipe-smoking and do not shun mildly alcoholic drinks!

Engaged couple at a party

The pipe, when being smoked, rests on the ground.

Drinking cup made from a stag's horn.

Growing Old

Even a gnome's life must come to an end. Over 400 years of age, the male rapidly becomes stiff and forgetful, though other gnomes still respect him. Eventually, the shriveled-up old man develops a tendency to wander. His wife displays the same symptoms, she being almost the same age herself. The housekeeping begins to suffer; the house starts to decay and becomes dirty and dark.

On one particular night, the aged couple does not return from their wandering. They have begun their journey to the Mountain of Death (never seen by human eyes)—and with the certainty of the migratory bird they will find it, if they are not attacked on the way by animals of prey.

As soon as they die, their birthday tree begins to get dead branches unless it is used by more than one gnome. (See TIMEKEEPING.)

Lives beyond 400 years or so have seldom been recorded, with the exception of a married couple in the Balkans who lived 550 years. But they were looked after for a great while by generations of a farming family, who placed a bowl of yogurt in the stable for them every day. They each had an olive tree on the Adriatic Sea.

Types of Gnomes

There are: woodland gnomes, dune gnomes, garden gnomes, house gnomes, farm gnomes, and Siberian gnomes.

Woodland Gnome

The woodland, or forest, gnome is probably the most common. But this is difficult to verify, as he is not fond of showing himself to man and has many escape routes. His physical appearance resembles that of the ordinary gnome.

Dune Gnome

The dune gnome is a fraction larger than the woodland gnome. He, too, avoids contact with man. His clothing is sometimes remarkably drab. The female of this gnome type does not wear gray clothes; hers are khaki-colored.

Garden Gnome

The garden gnome belongs to the general type. He lives in old gardens, even those hemmed in between the new houses of modern "model" cities. His nature is on the somber side, and he rather enjoys telling melancholy tales. If he begins to feel too closed in, he simply goes to the woods. But, as he is quite learned, he sometimes feels out of place there.

Farm Gnome

The farm gnome resembles the house gnome but is of a more constant nature and is conservative in all matters.

House Gnome

The house gnome is a special sort. He resembles an ordinary gnome but he has the most knowledge of mankind. Owing to the fact that he often inhabits historic old houses, he has seen both rich and poor, and heard a great deal. He speaks and understands man's language; gnome kings are chosen from his family.

The gnomes mentioned above are good-natured, always ready for a lark or to tease; they are never malevolent, with a few exceptions, of course. If a gnome is really wicked—which happens only once in a thousand—it is due to bad genes that result from crossbreeding in faraway places.

Siberian Gnome

The Siberian gnome has been the most affected by crossbreeding. He is centimeters larger than the European type and associates freely with trolls. In certain regions there is not a single gnome to be trusted. The Siberian gnome takes revenge for even the slightest offense by killing cattle, causing bad harvests, droughts, abnormally cold weather, and so forth.

The less said about him, the better.

Every now and then a gnome family will inhabit a windmill.

Timekeeping

Gnomes have their own secret way of telling time, based on cosmic oscillation. It is no trick at all for them to predict long-term periods of dry or wet weather, severe or mild winters. Excepting this, however, they use our method of timekeeping. Some of them have silver or gold watches. The cuckoo clock that hangs in every gnome's house is the traditional wedding present given to the groom on his wedding day.

A gnome keeps track of his age through the growth of an acorn planted in the ground on his day of birth. (A lime tree planted on the same day somewhere in the vicinity will do just as well.)

Cuckoo Clock

As soon as the tree is large enough, it is marked with runic writing by the parents. At the same time a copy is carved in a flat stone or on a clay tablet, and this plaque is given to the gnome in question on his 25th birthday; he keeps it in a secret place for the rest of his life. Very large old oak trees sometimes bear the runic writings of more than one gnome born in the same year.

Gnomes visit their birthday tree yearly on Midsummer Eve and add a mark to the runic script. Sometimes they even live under the tree, so they can easily check on their age when in doubt.

Gnomes snicker at man's superstition

"When the tree's big and wide
The planter has died"

They are extremely upset if their tree is cut down; but if that occurs they quickly plant a new one and continue to count on it.

Their adopted trees are never struck by lightning, storm, or disease. The tree begins to decay only when the gnome dies, unless, of course, it is shared by other gnomes who are still living.

Birthdays are not celebrated. The gnome sets aside an indefinite period of several weeks for quiet parties, during which he dwells on the fact that he is a year older. Upon request from faraway friends, he will extend these birthday weeks for an unlimited period.

Courtship, Marriage and the Family

When he is about 100, the male gnome begins to think of marriage; a small number do, however, remain single. The youthful gnome then begins to search for his girl. In doing so, he sometimes has to travel great distances because gnomes are few and far between and the number of eligible girls of his age not related to him is very limited. Plump womenfolk, round of form, are the favorite. If he does find one, he attempts to win her with all sorts of small attentions. After an agreement is reached with the in-laws to be, he will marry her. His house is given a rigorous inspection beforehand by his future father-in-law.

The Wedding

is a simple ceremony (except among the nobility)

At midnight, under the bride's birthday tree, the young
couple, attended by parents and close friends, promise to
be eternally true.*

*This always occurs under a full moon. If the moon disappears behind a
cloud, causing darkness to fall on the festivities, they don luminous caps
with a short train full of glowworms to ensure a few hours' light. These
caps have been in the family for generations and are worn only on such
occasions because this is tough work for the glowworms.

After the ceremony, the memorable occasion and date are engraved on an ornamental stone. Then the party retires to the young couple's house, where the stone is solemnly walled up. (The new house was furnished years before.)

After a festive dinner, the newlyweds leave for their honeymoon trip.

The honeymoon trip was discussed long in advance, with animals used for transportation and safety — wild geese, → swans, storks...

...foxes, otters, and in Siberia wolves — all do their share.

The honeymoon couple spend their nights in hollow tree trunks, rabbit holes, or uninhabited birds' nests. On their return trip, they visit the gnome palace and pay their respects to their king and queen, who like to know all their subjects by name.

Out of this union,
a pair of twins
is born, in the usual manner. Pregnancy lasts 12 months. Long ago—more than 1,000 years—families were much larger, sometimes 10 or 12 children. Due to a certain intervention, about which gnomes decline to speak, this is no longer the case.

The twins may be 2 boys, 2 girls, or a boy and a girl.

Since no deaths are caused by illness, the total gnome population remains about the same, with a slight tendency to decrease owing to the few who stay single and others who have fallen victim to accident or animals of prey. Gnome children wet the bed until they are 12; they live with their parents until they are 100 years old.

The gnome father leaves the upbringing of daughters to their mothers and limits his fatherly attentions to occasional horserides on his knee,
storytelling,
carving wooden animals

and playing games with them.

As soon as his son (or sons) turns 13, the gnome father takes him outside to teach him the many things every gnome should Know:

KNOWLEDGE of mushrooms and herbs; how to distinguish between edible and poisonous plants, and friendly or dangerous animals.

How to increase his **Running speed** (to that of a hare.)

Methods of escape (in open terrain the so-called "heel slapping," or zig-zag method, and in wooded areas the use of mole tunnels, rabbit warrens, underground water courses, etc.)

Further, he is taught to handle the **Divining rod** which every gnome uses to trace water, locate treasures, and find earth rays.

Another important skill passed from father to son is **Whistling** shrilly — and loud enough to be heard at great distances — to warn of impending danger!

Gnome boys are also taught how to use a metal mirror to reflect the sun or moon's rays and flash messages when there is danger about.

gnome boy of 81, already beginning to turn gray ↘

Indoors, the youthful gnome is taught all the tricks of the **Woodworking and Painting** trades.

At community forges and potteries (located in central areas in the woods and fields), the gnome student masters several trades—they feel that one can never learn enough.

When he is 75 years old, the son is introduced by his father to the members of the Regional Council, a few of whom he already knows. This initiation sometimes degenerates into a sort of hazing ritual that can cause him a few uncomfortable nights, but he eventually is rewarded with entry in the register and general good fellowship.

Girls are instructed by their mothers and neighbor women in the homely arts.

They learn cooking, spinning, knitting, and how to identify animals of prey— in short, everything a woman should know about running a home.

One of her favorite pastimes is cuddling and bottle-feeding the neighborhood baby rabbits, especially if their mothers have been killed by hunters or animals.

After the children leave home, the gnome father is again alone with just his wife—and this, after a brief period of readjustment, becomes quite agreeable. Family life need not be less harmonious because children leave home. If there is reason for celebration, gnomes from near and far will join in the festivities at the drop of a hat; the gossiping, drinking, eating, and dancing may last for days.

Gnome dancing is of the Yugoslavian sort: they move in circles, and there is much boot slapping and hand clapping. The gnome women deck themselves out with blossoms or berry-bearing twigs.

Special dress for dance parties:

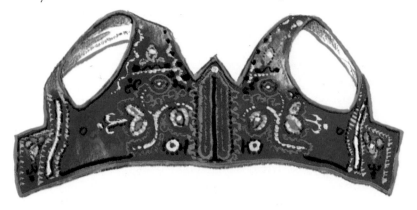

Attractive embroidered **Bolero** and "folk dancing" slippers.

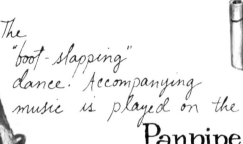

The "boot-slapping" dance. Accompanying music is played on the

Panpipe, String instruments

(on rare occasions the violin), **flutes** carved from wood or hollowed rabbit bones, and a mouse-skin **Drum.**

They sing along with the music very softly.

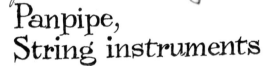

On warm spring evenings they love to let the thrush lead the singing, then they follow with their own **dreamy, melancholic variations** on that theme.

Later, when the thrush and blackbird are asleep, they thrill to the louder, more metallic, sounds of the nightingale.

Housebuilding

Gnome houses differ in style and location, depending on the area where they are built.

The woodland and garden gnomes live under large, old trees. The dune gnome makes use of renovated rabbit holes or else houses himself under pine-tree roots. If sand drifts expose parts of his house he covers them with pine-cone scales.

In earlier days, when the subsoil water in the dunes was higher, large pine trees produced grapefruit-size pine cones, and their scales made excellent roof tiles. Unfortunately, these trees exist now only in limited numbers.

Although the house gnome may have his residence in a garden, he can nestle down just as well between the walls of a house.

The farm gnome may live under the haystack—but here he must always be on the lookout for polecats. He sometimes resides in one of the supply sheds on a farm or under sloping planks or poles leaning against farmhouse walls—which through neglect sometimes remain in that position for twenty years. But owing to the danger of a polecat, cat, or rat, farm gnomes usually choose a well-built little house and make their home under the roof tiles, or somewhere in the stables.

Hidden
Entrance

The Tree House

The gnome starts building his house 15 to 20 years before his marriage. First, he looks around for a spot in a garden or in the woods where lichen or beard moss grows. This indicates clean air, for otherwise these moss species would die (exhaust fumes, etc.). Using the divining rod, he makes certain there are no earth rays in the area.

Under the first stairway we find a polecat trap, a folding trapdoor. The gnomes (and their visitors) who come in and out are too light to set the trap in action, but the ferret, polecat, weasel, or rat, greedily entering the hole, immediately tumbles below through the trapdoor (after thorough punishment they are set free).

How the polecat trap works

Next he looks for two oak trees not too far apart (if need be, he will use beech trees). Under the roots of one tree, on the south side, he makes a staircase, then digs a hidden entrance. From here he tunnels (with the help of a rabbit; see further on) a crooked horizontal passageway under the trunk; this descends steeply after a short distance. Then he tunnels horizontally to the second tree, and rises to where the rabbit has prepared a hollow for the house itself under the tree trunk (dug in such a fashion as not to damage the second tree in any way).

The main direction of the house will be north–south. Where the passage rises, he builds an ascending stairway, with a bannister. A gong and hammer are hung nearby. A welcome mat is placed at the bottom of the stairs.

A the gong
B front door
C boot room
D well with bucket
E cage with watch-cricket
F dowry chest
G insulation layer of doe's hair
H drying attic for fruit, etc.

I chimney and air vent
J carved portraits
K door to washroom
L sleeping alcove
M basket of pine needles
N toilet
O chest of dried leaves

Boot room

The first area the gnome partitions off is the

He begins by planing the wallboards until they are completely straight and smooth; then he waterproofs the floor. Next, he insulates the ceiling and walls with doe hair, wool, and moss fiber, all bound together with tough blades of grass. The planks may now be nailed to the walls. The floor is made from trodden-down loam or planks. (Needless to say, he saws the planks from tree trunks himself. He has years of time for that.)

The Living room

After the boot room, we have the living room, with extensions for three bed
alcoves (one for father and mother, another for two children, and a third for
guests). A corner is reserved for the kitchen; spaces for a bathroom, a fireplace,
a hobby area, and a very roomy toilet. This enormous living area is also planed
smooth, and it is thickly insulated with wool, hair, and fiber; walls and floors
are covered with planks and beams. Father's help is indispensable.

the **Chimney**

(also an air vent)
The chimney of the future
stove is connected to
a woodpecker's hole.

Moles are good friends of the gnome. Here, one digs a vertical hole, meters deep, under the future toilet. If, every time after use, dried leaves are thrown down the hole, the sewage need not be removed and in time may produce nourishment for the tree. In former times, the wall of the vertical tunnel was lined with woven twigs to prevent its collapsing. Today, round piping sections of baked clay are used.

Mole

In a corner of the boot room the mole digs a second vertical tunnel. This well will connect to a spring, pure subsoil water, or an underground stream. The gnome then builds a stone wall around the well opening. Gnomes make no cement but sometimes get it from men in exchange for something or other. A mixture of mud, ash, and cow dung is generally used to cement stones together. The walls of the tunnel are lined with earthenware pipe sections to prevent crumbling and pollution. The construction of underground tunnels is one of the most time-consuming occupations of the gnome builder.

When the house is finished –
  after years of **patient, steady, skillful labor** –
it looks like this, starting below the second tree:

At the top of the second stairway we find a heavy,
attractively carved front door, which opens to the boot
room. The middle section of the door is composed of an
equally attractive iron grille against which an inside door is
attached. This inside door is mostly left open to allow a
light air current to pass through the house from the
hallway. This draft is produced either by the wind outside
the tunnel or by suction from the fireplace.

In another corner of the boot room we
find the well with a bucket on a pulley.
Along the wall are more buckets and a
tub; various pots and bottles stand on a
work table, above which hangs the cage
of the watch-cricket; he has sharp
ears and announces any creature
approaching from the outside passage.
The gnomes usually find the crickets
lodged in cracks between stones of old
chimneys. They care for them well and
give them abundant meals.

The bride's wedding present, a dowry chest, is placed in another corner of the boot room. The chest rests on low feet and is beautifully carved and painted. Departing visitors are given presents that have been stored in the chest. These may be natural things, useful implements, or writings to be pondered upon, such as an odd sentence, a poem, or a profound proverb that may take a long time to understand.

Dowry chest

A second door, opposite the front door, leads to the

Living room ➡

Upon entering, we see an oblong table on the right. At one side of it is a corner seat against the wall; on the other side are father's and mother's chairs (children *stand* at the table). A Christmas centerpiece remains on the table all the year round.

Farther to the right we have the play and hobby room, which also contains the guest alcove—big enough for two. The trapdoor built into the floor connects to an underground passage. In the play area or under the table is the basket for the field-mouse family that keeps the house free of insects and vermin.*

The gnome keeps 3 or 4; they are tame and house-trained like man's dog. The young ones are amusing playmates for the gnome children. When they are grown they are either exchanged for others or set free.

Because of the good care that they receive they are convivial companions. It is a pity that their life-span is so short.

*The Russet Field mouse is 9–13.5 cm. long. Tail length 4–6 cm. (80 rings). Its back is red-brown, stomach white. The feet are also white. The head is short and blunt; large eyes and ears. An excellent digger and climber. Every year the female gives birth to 2 to 8 young, who open their eyes after 10 days. Pregnancy lasts 17–18 days. Life-span: 2–3 years.

Russet Field Mouse

To catch small, annoying underground flies, a bog plant (*Pinguicula vulgaris*) is hung from the ceiling; the flies are caught on its sticky leaves.

Beyond the playroom is the door leading to the toilet room. The door is beautiful—sometimes inlaid with precious stones—but the comfortable "throne" inside is even more beautiful. Neither labor nor cost is spared in its carving and painting. The gnome takes his time when using this room and meanwhile occupies himself with handcraft. Toilet paper, made with the aid of the paper wasp, hangs next to the "throne." Alongside stands a tall stone jar full of dried leaves to throw down the hole afterward.

Toilet

The Large Stove

Back in the living room we find a neatly stacked woodpile for fuel. In a tall basket are fragrant pine needles used as an air refresher. (The gnome is very skilled in lighting fire; he uses dried tinder fungus, which grows on beech trees. With two flints he strikes the necessary sparks.)

Then we have the large, gaily painted chimney, facing north, and underneath it the stove, which is used for cooking and providing warmth. Spoons, pokers, pipes, and candle holders hang on the chimney walls.

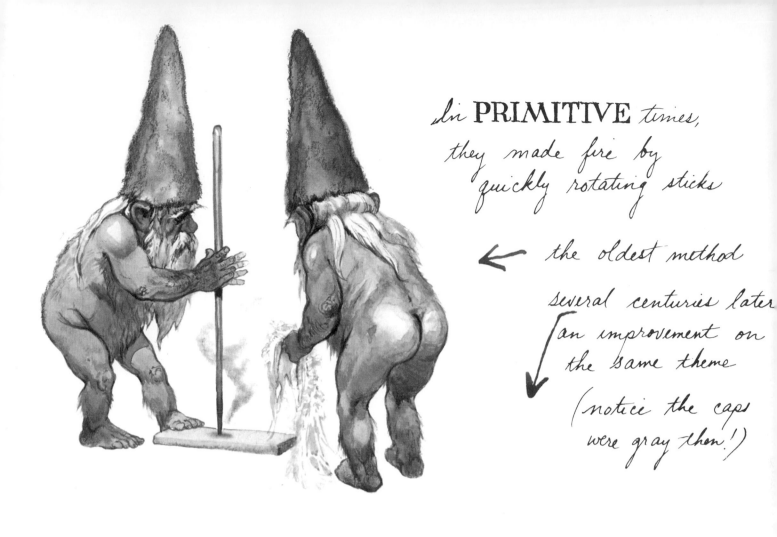

In PRIMITIVE times,
they made fire by
quickly rotating sticks

← the oldest method

several centuries later
⌐an improvement on
the same theme
(notice the caps
were gray then!)

Gnomes made oil paint from earth pigments* long before men (who invented and used it just before and during the time of the Van Eyck brothers—about 1400). Gnomes use paint for decorating furniture and the interiors of their houses; they do not use it to paint pictures. Instead, they carve portraits of their ancestors, loved ones, or celebrities.

*From earth and clay—cleansed, then mixed with oil. It holds up well in paintings and comes in ochers, umbers, burnt sienna, terra-cotta, Vandyke brown, etc.

As counterpart to the toilet room, there is an equally large bathroom. The wrought-iron tub is filled with buckets of water heated on the stove. Sometimes there is a shower connected to a reservoir of rainwater in the attic. The bathwater drain is connected by a sloping tunnel to the vertical sewer line. In the bathroom, mirrors of polished silver, made with patience and devotion—and just as effective as glass mirrors—hang on the walls.

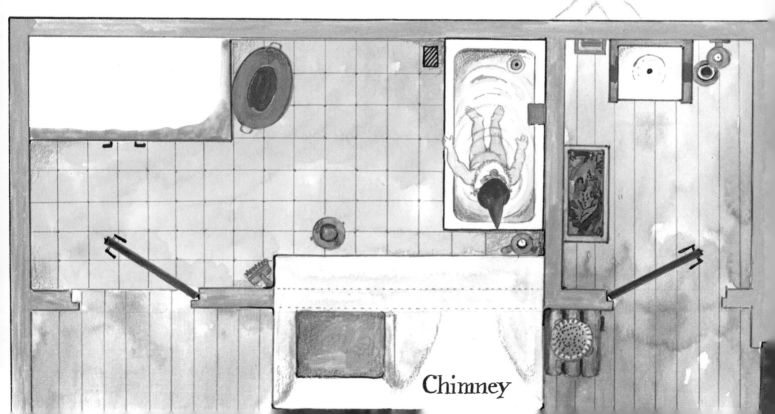

sewer

Chimney

Continuing in a clockwise direction, we come to the side wall where the family alcoves (cupboard beds) are situated, with a bench under each alcove for stepping up. Carved portraits and bed warmers hang on the alcove walls. Between the alcoves is a neat row of storage drawers.

Finally, returning to the living-room door, we find the cuckoo clock, found in every gnome residence. Every gnome bridegroom receives one when he gets married, as already noted.

The living room has a double ceiling. The space between is used for drying fruit; it can be reached via a small ladder and trapdoor. Hooks, for hanging a cradle in the living room, are attached to the lower beams.

The interior layout of every gnome house depends more or less on the position of the roots of the tree under which it is built. Some gnomes prefer a deep-lying house without windows, while others prefer a high window somewhere in a sloping roof—especially in soggy forests where deep building is difficult.

Wax candles are used to obtain light. The gnomes make them from beeswax (see HOME INDUSTRY).

Being on good terms with rabbit and mole has mutual benefits, apart from the joy of harmonious contact. These gray and black-velvet toilers patiently dig all the tunnels and passages needed by the gnome. A special advantage here is that they will never inadvertently dig up a gnome house because they know exactly where each one is situated.

In return for its efforts in tunneling, a gnome will always warn a mole if he discovers a mole trap in one of his passages, which the mole might otherwise not notice until it was too late. The gnome also advises rabbits to remain inside when there is hunting in the vicinity; furthermore, he keeps the rabbit company during his last miserable hours if the poor creature is stricken by myxomatosis. The rabbit's death cannot, of course, be prevented, but the gnome can mercifully give him pain-killing opium drops to ease his passing.

All gnome houses have, in one of the walls or in the floor, a special opening—covered with a cloth—connected to a rabbit hole. This opening also serves as an escape route in extreme emergencies.

Any part of the gnome house that protrudes from under the roots—for example, small storerooms in high subsoil water or drift-sand areas—is tiled with pine-cone scales, as mentioned earlier. Moss or lichen later grows over it, camouflaging it well.

The Third Tree

Under a third tree close to the house, the stock and supply rooms are built. Here the gnome stores his grain, beans, seeds, potatoes, and nuts. These supplies are indispensable, especially during long, severe winters. Incidentally, the gnome does not mind helping out any poor hungry wretch that has run out of food. The supply and stock rooms under the third tree are sometimes connected to the house, but not always.

A hilarious sight is a gnome busy filling his storeroom while behind his back a hamster is busy emptying it. Naturally, when this is detected, a lot of bickering follows.

Hamster

Gnome dwellings in and around farms and old houses, although adapted to their surroundings, are usually of the same basic pattern. Again we find the polecat trap near the entrance. Rainwater is cleverly trapped in roof gutters and stored in a reservoir. The toilet and bath water is generally drained off into the manure gutters of the cowshed.

A variant of the basic gnome home is the willow house, which usually serves as a holiday house. Windswept (sometimes almost lying flat) pollard willows and poplars are used for this purpose. The gnome occupies about a third of such a hollow trunk. Ducks also nest in these trees and apparently feel greatly reassured by the gnomes' presence—especially while they are off their guard, bathing or eating.

Daily Routine

After sunset the gnome house comes to life (even without windows, they know when it begins to get dark – and besides, the field mice begin to fiddle about then). The lady of the house steps out of the alcove bed, puts on her slippers, and shuffles off to the stove, where she gets the fire under way by adding dry leaves to the embers.

Next, she puts a couple of pails of water on to heat (if her husband wants a bath, that is) and a kettle on for tea. She then goes to the bathroom to make herself presentable.

When she leaves the bathroom,
her husband waits a few
minutes, then pokes his feet out
of the alcove bed (sometimes with
morning mumbles and grumbles).

He then steps into his slippers,
and hangs his nightshirt and nightcap on
a handsome wrought-iron peg. He looks on approv-
ingly as his wife empties hot water into the tub;
testing the temperature, he then steps into his bath.

In bathing, he takes a couple of handfuls
of dried **SOAPWORT** (Saponaria
Officinalis) from a tray hanging on the
wall and splashes it about in the
water to produce an abundance of
suds.

While mother and father are thus occupied, the children set the table.

In the meantime, father dries himself.

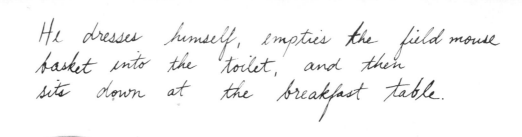

He dresses himself, empties the field mouse basket into the toilet, and then sits down at the breakfast table.

Breakfast is as follows :

A Mint tea
Rose-hip tea
Linden-blossom tea
Jasmine tea
} *any of these*

Rose hips

B Eggs *from small songbirds*

C Mushrooms *(various sorts as illustrated)*

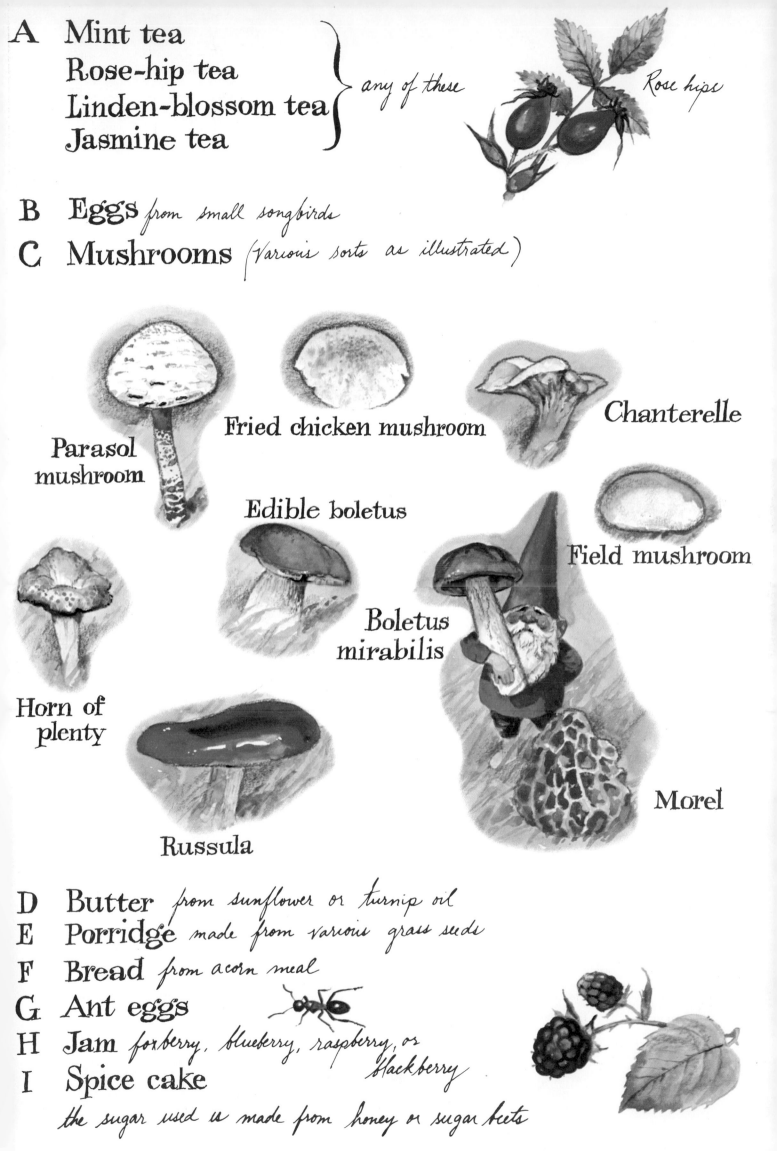

Parasol mushroom

Fried chicken mushroom

Chanterelle

Edible boletus

Field mushroom

Horn of plenty

Boletus mirabilis

Russula

Morel

D Butter *from sunflower or turnip oil*
E Porridge *made from various grass seeds*
F Bread *from acorn meal*
G Ant eggs
H Jam *foxberry, blueberry, raspberry, or blackberry*
I Spice cake

the sugar used is made from honey or sugar beets

His wife prepares a snack for his night journey— a hollowed acorn filled with tea and a bag of biscuits. The biscuits, baked from various grass seeds, are a hearty meal in themselves.

He lights his first pipe, waits until his wife has cleared away the breakfast things, and then they discuss the coming nightly activities or problems concerning the children.

On leaving the house, he pats the watch-cricket, walks through the long passage, climbs up the short stairway and "checks out"* the terrain for a few minutes.

* Check Out = *prolonged careful listening and watching*

If it is not yet
dark enough, the
gnome waits beside a friendly rabbit until deeper
darkness falls...

Anything may happen, depending on what he encounters or what his particular job for the evening may be. He could go to the forge, pottery, or

Sawmill

The roof tiles of these buildings are made from pine-cone scales.

Or, he may go to his herb garden and either sow seeds, weed, hoe, prune, or harvest.

He may take care of the firewood supply — or pick berries...

In short, everything that can be done during short, sultry summer nights, long, cold winter nights, velvet black or moonlit nights, rainy nights, etc.

If snow has fallen he straps on his long-distance skis. These are absolutely necessary, otherwise he would sink right into the snow, especially when it is fresh!

If his affairs do not cause him to spend the night elsewhere, the gnome returns home shortly before sunrise, where preparations for the main meal are in progress. (There are only two meals a day, not counting snacks of milk or porridge).

The main meal consists of:

hazelnuts
walnuts
beechnuts, etc.

mush-
rooms (see
<u>Breakfast</u>)

peas

beans

one small potato

all sorts of vegetables

applesauce,
    fruit, berries
      of all kinds,
    tubers and spices

beverages

The gnome eats no meat, and so he regularly partakes of the high protein plant vetch (Vicia sepium), which also contains a nourishing nectar in its leaves.

mead de
(fermented
honey)

fermented raspberries
(sometimes with too high a
alcoholic content, alas!)

nightcap:
spiced gin

dessert: preserves

Children are breast-fed for several years

His wife meanwhile spends the night (if she has babies) changing and washing diapers, ironing, rocking the cradle, breast-feeding and singing songs — or else playing games, cooking, knitting, weaving, dusting, making beds, chatting with the rabbits, passing the time of day with neighbor women, feeding the watch-cricket or grumbling at the field mice.

As the sun rises, the father gnome reads a chapter from the **SECRET BOOK.** This is respectfully listened to by all. After that, the doors are bolted, the fire extinguished, children put to bed, and the field mice silenced.

And so the sun rises above the gnome dwelling. The bedded-down gnomes
bid one another *slitzweitz* (their word for "goodnight"). There is muffled
giggling in the children's alcove for a while, snores gradually rise from the
parents' alcove, the field mice attempt to find a more comfortable sleeping
position in their basket, the kettle cools on the fireplace, and in the boot
room the watch-cricket contentedly chirps his one song. All is safe. Outside
villains may lurk; storms, thunder, rain may erupt; animals of prey may
abound. But above the sturdy gnome house a great tree stands erect; the
alert watch-cricket, mole, and rabbit will immediately give warning if
necessary. Nothing can possibly happen.

At every new moon the gnome awakes in the middle of the day. He steps
cautiously out of bed and fetches the large Family Book. He sits down at the
table and records any unusual events that may have occurred during the
previous four weeks. He uses ink made from the inky cap mushroom. The
book is delivered to the palace every so often for the king's perusal; it enables
him to keep abreast of the activities of his subjects.

Home Industry

Lighting

Gnome houses and underground passages are lighted with **candles** and **oil lamps**

Gnome houses and underground passages are lighted by candles and oil lamps. The gnome makes the candles himself from beeswax: he keeps his beehives—small colonies—in hidden places in the woods and fields. To furnish a new hive, he rolls thin, cell-patterned sheets of wax and sets them upright in the hive. (He makes the cell patterns by pressing hexagonal pipes onto the wax sheets.) The bees build further on this pattern. The cell walls are made of wax, which the bees (fewer than 20,000) "sweat" out from wax glands in their abdomens.

The raw material for wax is pollen, eaten by the bees. Eggs are laid in the cells and sealed off by birth membrane. After many births, the incubation cells eventually become black, owing to the constant traffic of the bees, and must be removed. The gnome turns the hive upside down and cuts out the old cells. He places them in a metal box with a drainage pipe attached underneath. The lid is made of a double plate of glass. This apparatus is set in the sun. Under the drainage pipe he places a candle mold with a wick hung in the middle. The temperature in the metal box rises rapidly in the sun's heat and before long the melted wax begins to flow from the pipe, filling the candle mold. Upon cooling, the candle shrinks and is easily removed from the mold, its wick already in place.

wax sheet

In melting wax for his candles, the gnome must, of course, be outside during the day, and expose himself to harsh sunlight, to which he is unaccustomed. For protection he wears **Sun goggles** (similar to those used by Eskimos) made from a small strip of wood with a narrow slit.

Ceramics

The gnome makes all his own crockery. The material used is natural clay.* There are three forms of water present in clay:

1. Water chemically bound to silicate.
2. Water sucked up hygroscopically by the clay.
3. Water added to make the clay soft and pliable.

After an object (for example, a dish) has been shaped by hand, the water is eliminated in reverse order. First, the water added by the gnome is dried out in the sun and wind; next, heat up to 150° C is used to eliminate the hygroscopic water; finally, the actual firing, with heat up to 800° C eliminates the water in the silicate. The resulting product contains only silicate and is hard and durable. It has also shrunk 20 to 40 percent.

Owing to the natural impurities present (mainly from oxides), the end product is a red-brown color.

If the gnome adds calcium the color becomes lighter, almost yellow. This type of earthenware is called terra-cotta.

The more natural silicates present (calcium, potassium, carbon, or sulphur), the less porous the product. To avoid excessive shrinkage in the kiln (which results in cracking), ground sand or limestone is added to the clay while it is being kneaded.

*Clay is composed of hydrous aluminum silicate together with various natural impurities.

Under the eternal drip.

In ancient days, bowls and other utensils were made by placing a pebble under a constantly dripping water source; eventually the waters' action eroded a hollow in the stone. Nowadays a potter's wheel is used with clay.

The wheel rotates via a pedal mechanism. Plates, pots, vases, cups, and bowls are fashioned this way.

Spouts and handles are attached later.

Before firing, decorative patterns are pressed into the wet clay with carved wooden stamps. Painting is done after baking.

Potter's Kiln

Baking pottery over an open fire or in a hole in the ground has long been replaced by the kiln. The firing process requires heat up to 800° C, and this can be obtained only in a closed oven.

Other household utensils, including cups and saucers, are manufactured by gnome craftsmen from hollowed-out deer antlers. Knife handles, forks, spoons, and buttons are also lovingly carved from antlers.

Glassblowing

Glass is obtained by melting rock crystals. All glass objects used by the gnome are of quartz glass—a much higher quality than ordinary glass. Quartz glass does not break in extreme heat or cold; it hardly ever cracks and has a natural sparkle. The blowing must occur under extremely high temperatures.

In order to color glass, the gnome liberally adds to the melted crystal the minerals amethyst, yellow topaz, agate, red heliotrope, and green plasma. He also makes marbles for the children from these stones.

The very clearest quartz glass is used for spectacles, telescopes, drinking glasses, and window panes. Variously colored or clear glass is used for indoor or outdoor lamps or lanterns. Interestingly, the lanterns are shaped in the form of a gnome's head (with a cap, of course).

Metalwork

Gold, silver, copper, and iron are used. Gold and silver have no monetary value for the gnome, but he gladly and frequently uses them because of their durability in all types of weather and their appealing luster. There are large supplies of precious metal in royal homes and elsewhere (the origin of which is not certain), and every gnome may take as much as he needs.

The same applies to copper. This metal is collected in its natural state in Sweden and Hungary and then transported to central depots.

Iron is obtained from melting hematite, an ore that contains Fe_2O_3 (red-brown ferric oxide). The furnace, a round stone cylinder about 30 cm. high, is filled with layers of charcoal and finely beaten iron ore. When the furnace is lit, the fire is powerfully fanned with a series of bellows. After some time, the iron melts out and the liquid metal can be poured off. After various purification and remelting processes, it can be fashioned into wrought or cast iron.

The method for casting utility objects of gold, silver, copper, or iron is the cire-perdue method, an ancient process still in use. First, a wax model of the object required is shaped, then it is covered with clay, in which a small hole is made. The clay is heated until it hardens. In the meantime the wax melts and drains away through the hole, leaving a cavity inside the clay mold that is exactly the shape of the desired object. (This is why the process is called cire-perdue, or "lost-wax.") Molten metal is then poured into the empty clay mold. After cooling, the clay form is broken and discarded, and the finished piece stands revealed, requiring only polishing.

the
lost-wax
method

Carpentry

The gnome is a born carpenter and joiner. He makes all his own furniture—cupboards, chairs, benches, and so on—without using a single nail. Everything is constructed with dovetail joints, wooden dowels, and glue. Little metal hardware is used; even cupboard doors are hinged by vertical wooden pins at top and bottom.

Constructing **bird houses** is a labor of love for the gnome.
All are made to measure. We see them hanging in isolated places in the woods. Out of gratitude, nesting birds allow the gnome to examine their eggs and take home any unfertilized specimens to eat.

When walking in the woods, please take note of any tiny holes you may see in tree trunks.
They are caused by the gnome's special "pole-climbing" shoes.

FLAX or LINSEED

Gnome housewives make all the family clothing. They weave flax into linen.

Clothmaking

Gnomes plant flaxseed in a secret garden, taking care to place seeds very close together to prevent the stalks' branching out. After a period of growth, all unripe yellow stalks are removed. These are then rippled to eliminate the seeds.

The stalks are now subjected to a rotting-fermentation process and then dried. Flax fibers are then separated through a metal comb, flattened, and rolled into balls.

The gnome wife spins the prepared flax into thread very finely, and after twining it, weaves it on her loom.

Doe hair is used to make wool (especially when it is strong and stiff). The gnome wife knits underwear, stockings, socks, gloves, and scarves. **Doe hair** is readily available, of course, to the woodland gnome.

For softer articles, the gnome is permitted to take as much loose hair from a rabbits' nest as he requires...

Stray pieces of sheep wool found blowing in the fields or caught on barbed-wire fences are used to make heavy blankets and sweaters.

Each of these types of wool is washed, oiled, dried, combed, hackled, spun, twisted, and knitted or woven.

WOOL DYEING

of the various sorts proceeds as follows:

for **RED** use Hemp agrimony

for **YELLOW** use Sawwort (*Serratula tinctoria*) or Columbine leaves

for Blue use Indigo (*Isatis tinctoria*)
(the powder derived from this indigo plant is originally copper-red but turns blue through oxidation.)

The gnome wife can also make wool from **Thistle Down** which produces fuzzy balls from which fibers may be carded.

Basketry and Weaving

the so-called "round weave" for circular forms

circular woven floor mat

plaited basketry

Woven fence (the technique speaks for itself.)

← Old weaving loom

improved ↑
model

young woman
string weaving

a weaving →
tool. The "even" threads
are moved up and
down

Birch Bark

After endless pounding, birch bark becomes soft enough to make coats and shoes.
(These items are also, of course, → stitched together from doe-hair felt or stiff moss fibers.

LEATHER is not readily available. The skin used must come from mice, squirrels, rabbits, or other animals who have died an unnatural death — for example, a car accident, severe frost, pesticides, or fighting.

Leather is also used for making pants, tobacco pouches, boots, shoes, purses, and belts — and sometimes even door hinges.

A few gnomes even own a **silkworm stable** but the silk they gather is mainly used to supply the palace.

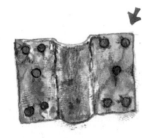

Relations with Animals

Obviously, gnomes maintain close contact with animals. They are, shall we say, on the same wavelength.

This means, of course, that the gnome speaks their language and understands their problems. All animals — even the troublesome ones already mentioned, such as the polecat, rat, etc. — feel safe with the gnome and are trusted by him. The cat, however, remains an exception — especially the wild domestic cat, who is not a member of the natural animal world and is completely unreliable.

Gnomes are often sought out by even such large animals as the wolf, lynx, bear, fox, and wild boar (who are by no means favorites). They know where to find the gnome when they need him. In return, they usually do his bidding without too much sulking.

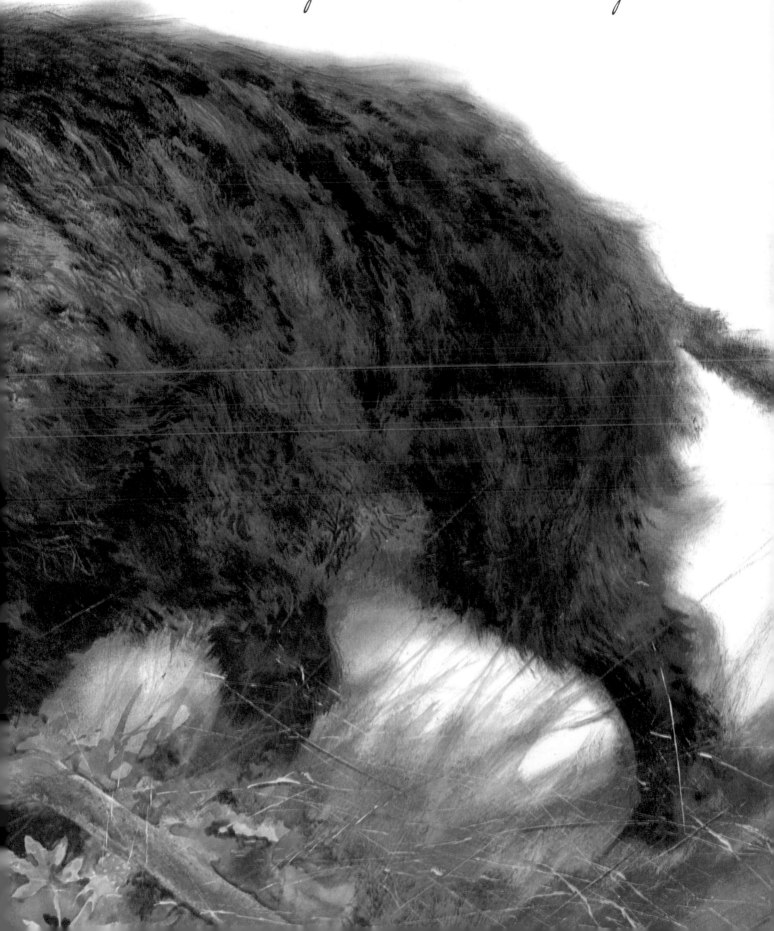

Some examples of Gnome "First Aid":

Indeed, the gnome is indispensable to the animal world. His intellect and technical skills allow him to do things that animals are incapable of doing themselves.

Foxes and other animals can become irritated by ticks embedded in the skin on their heads or other areas difficult for them to reach. When they try to scrape the tick away against a tree, the insect's head remains under the skin, causing inflammation. The gnome waits until the tick is sleeping, then he twists it out quickly in counterclockwise direction.

When two stags become "entangled" during a fight, that is to say, when their antlers become inextricably entwined (mostly because of extra points or abnormal protrusions), the gnome saws them apart. The poor devils, by then usually half starved, are free once more. Antlers have no feeling, so the whole operation is painless.

When a cow or goat has "the sharps," that is to say, a sharp object lodged in its paunch (for example, a paring knife it may have swallowed, a piece of glass, or wire), the gnome will operate to remove it. Normally, the farmer or owner first discovers the animal's distress and he calls the veterinary; but in neglected cases or when the owner is too poor to pay the animal doctor, gnomes have been known to take over.

(The hair on the flank is shaved and the skin opened via a small incision. The three-layered muscle lining of the stomach is then pushed open in three directions and clamped. After the peritoneum has been opened, the side lining of the stomach becomes visible. After some searching, the sharp object is located and only a negligible incision is required to remove it. The stomach, peritoneum, stomach wall, and skin are stitched up in layers.)

If a rabbit caught in a snare has the presence of mind not to become overexcited and simply to wait patiently, a gnome will soon come along to save him. With a file and pincers, any gnome can manage to lift even the most deeply embedded wire from a rabbit's throat and file it through.

Among other services rendered to rabbits by gnomes, we have already mentioned warnings of impending danger from humans and the wonderful comfort given to rabbits sick with myxomatosis during their last miserable hours.

In addition, gnomes have a way of healing broken limbs (from shotgun or rifle fire or being run over by a car) that is nothing short of miraculous; so much so that one cannot help but suspect the influence of a superior being. Animals wounded in these ways usually withdraw into a thicket for 14 days or so, to allow time for the gnomes to care for them.

Gnomes amuse themselves greatly
by refereeing early-morning
fights between **Black cocks**

Due to greedy swallowing, acorns and sometimes larger items become lodged in a goose's throat. By using external force with his hands to turn the acorn internally, the gnome helps the nut to glide down into the goose's stomach.

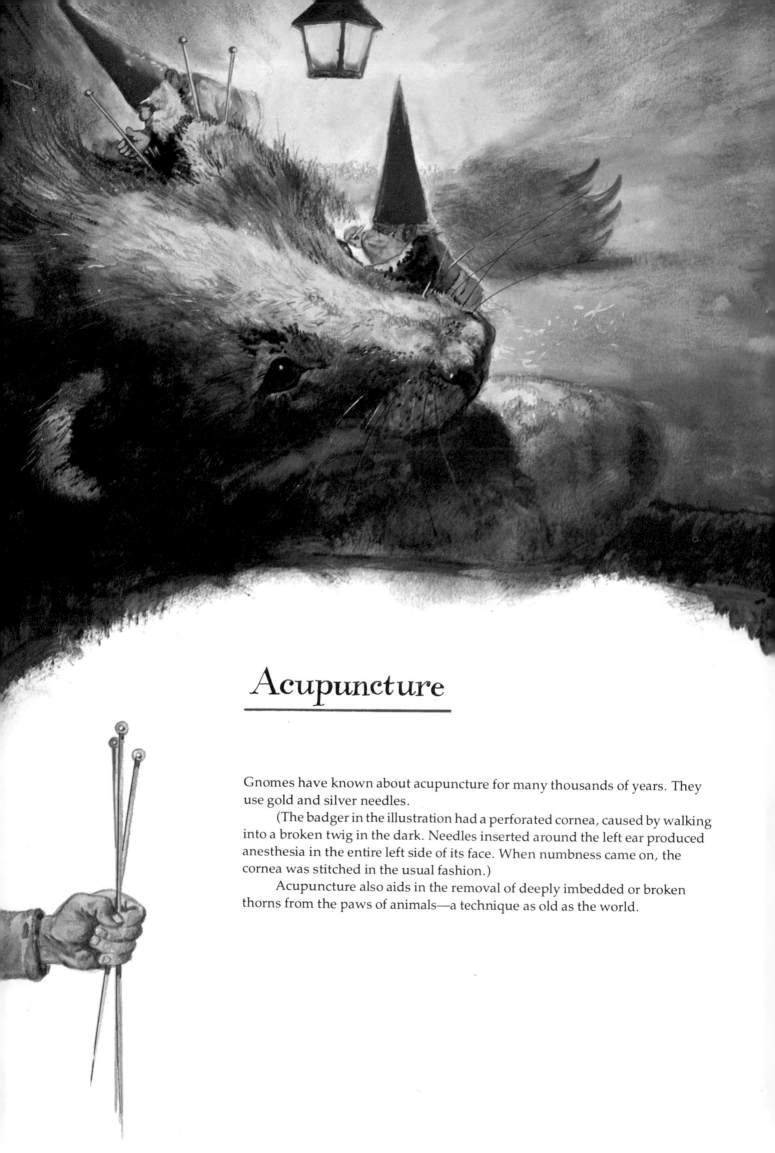

Acupuncture

Gnomes have known about acupuncture for many thousands of years. They use gold and silver needles.

(The badger in the illustration had a perforated cornea, caused by walking into a broken twig in the dark. Needles inserted around the left ear produced anesthesia in the entire left side of its face. When numbness came on, the cornea was stitched in the usual fashion.)

Acupuncture also aids in the removal of deeply imbedded or broken thorns from the paws of animals—a technique as old as the world.

Horses in a stable or meadow
will never step on a gnome!
(Neither do cows or other large
animals.) Without fear, the
gnome can walk about be-
tween horses' legs or even
sleep under them.

Sometimes a deer's antlers become entangled with a piece of wire broken from a fence — or a strand of barbed wire or twisted branch becomes lodged in the antlers. The gnome not only finds this unattractive, but knows that it may cause the deer some danger, and he only too willingly removes the foreign matter.

Squirrels

Squirrels often forget many of the places where they have hidden their nuts for the winter. In long or severe winters this could mean starvation. The gnome of the vicinity, with his infallible memory, will always come to the rescue.

Spiders

Spiders are not especially friends of the gnome; but a gnome will never destroy a web, because that might bring bad luck.

Otters

The gnome makes use of the *otter* to transport him over streams, rivers, or other bodies of water. Swimming and giggling constantly, the otter ferries the gnome to the other side. (Swimming is too risky for gnomes because certain fish are too "fond" of them. True, a gnome could use a bark boat, but these are not at his disposal in every area.)

The old children's rhyme "Ladybug, ladybug, fly away home, Your house is on fire . . .," which makes her actually fly away, originated with gnome children.

The **Mouflon** is a wild sheep imported from Sardinia and Corsica. Because there is often not sufficient stony matter in the moorlands of his new country, his hooves do not wear down as they should and they take on the dimensions of Persian slippers! The gnome saws them off and files them into shape.

The gnome feels the **responsibility** to supply small rodents with food from his storage during the long, severe winter.

Constriction in a deer's chest may be caused by "throat" horseflies. The horsefly lays its eggs in the deer's nose and the larvae work their way into the throat and nestle there. The gnome removes the intruders with a "throat" horsefly pincer.

Throatfly larva actual size

The pincer

A hen pheasant can only count up to three. When she has to cross a ditch with her brood, she waits until the third chick catches up, then continues on her way— leaving the others (who could easily drown) behind her. The gnome helps by finding the abandoned chicks during the twilight hours, locating the mother, and then placing the babes under her.

The gnome does so many favors for wild
boars and deer that they do not begrudge the few
potatoes he takes from the feeding places that farmers
set out for them.

Polecat

gnomes have a difficult time accepting polecats because they know that they paralyze living frogs and save them for later eating. The gnome is told about this as a child, and all through his life he has an anxiety that the same fate may await him!

Games

Swinging

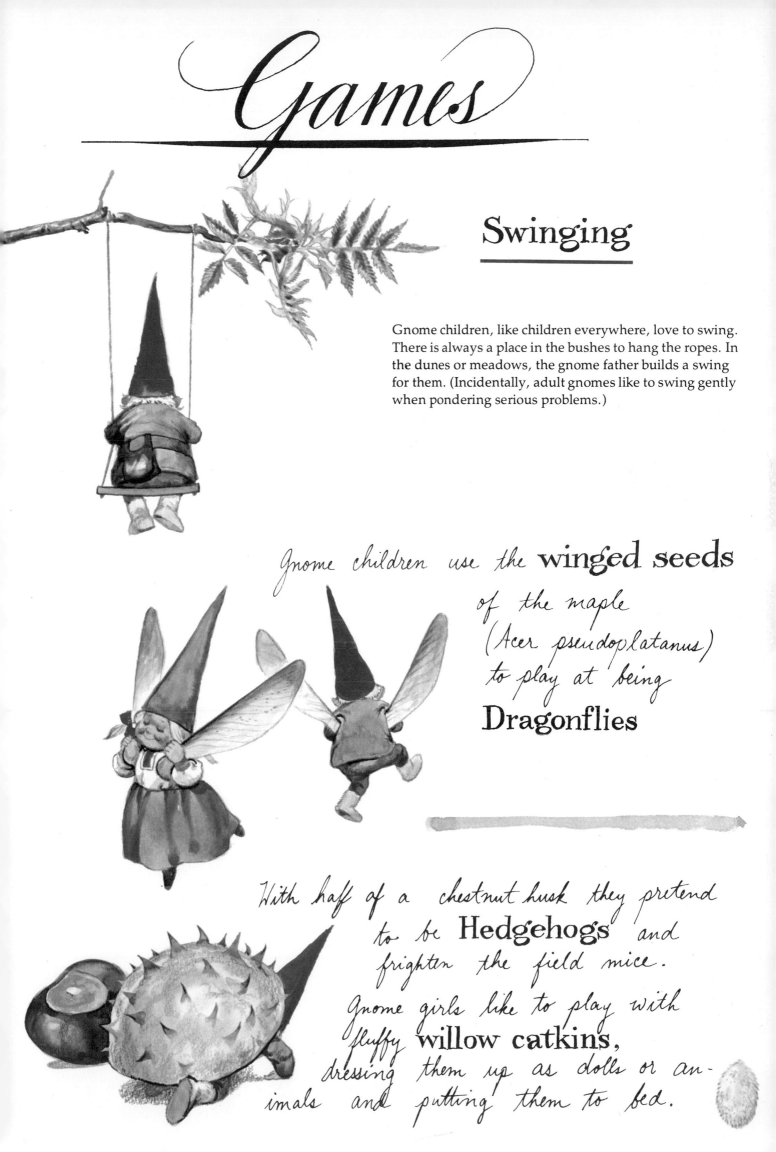

Gnome children, like children everywhere, love to swing. There is always a place in the bushes to hang the ropes. In the dunes or meadows, the gnome father builds a swing for them. (Incidentally, adult gnomes like to swing gently when pondering serious problems.)

Gnome children use the **winged seeds** of the maple (Acer pseudoplatanus) to play at being **Dragonflies**

With half of a chestnut husk they pretend to be **Hedgehogs** and frighten the field mice.

Gnome girls like to play with fluffy **willow catkins**, dressing them up as dolls or animals and putting them to bed.

Blowpipes are made from the hollow stems of the flute weed (Anthriscus vulgaris) or parsnip (Pastinaca sativa).

They play **Marbles** with pebbles or clay balls made by their fathers.
They also play **Territory** — with a pocket knife.
Bowling is played at the edge of a meadow with dried, odorless rabbit droppings; and a respectful audience of rabbits looks on.

Tug of War

Soccer using a Snowberry

Red rover, Jump rope, Blindman's buff,

Kite flying *(when mother and father aren't looking)* using a Junebug
or bumblebee.

Dressing up *as elves, witches father, mother,
king, queen, etc.*

Balance board

with the most perfect and smoothest boards

Checkers, Flip-the-cap

Authors

Bur-throwing *(to tease animals and
people)*

Gnome parchesi.

Language

Among themselves gnomes speak their own language. But since we come in contact only with solitary gnomes, we never hear it. (They can become very difficult if asked about their language.) It is certain, however, that animals understand it. "Goodnight" is *slitzweitz*, and "thank you" is *te diews*. We did not progress much beyond these few words mainly because the gnomes master man's languages perfectly. And if they cannot place a word, they immediately ask its meaning. Their written language is the ancient runic script.

"Slitzweitz" = Goodbye

Other Twilight and Night Beings

Elves, Goblins, House Ghosts, Trolls, Dwarfs, River Spirits, Wood Nymphs, Mountain Nymphs, Uldras.

Because the above-mentioned are often confused with gnomes, detailed descriptions follow:

Elves

An elf is an airy spirit of nature, who loves carefree dancing and playing stringed instruments. Elves live underground, or sometimes in or on top of water (preferably a spring), or sometimes even in the air (or in the branches of high trees). Now and then they take on an animal image. They are not malevolent by nature, but sometimes the consequences of their teasing have been serious (for example, causing people to become lost in the marshes) but it is not at all intentional. There are male, female, and sexless elves. Most of them have wings.
Size: from 10 to 30 cm.
Intelligence: sharply focused, but high.

Goblins

Goblins grow to 30 cm. in length; dark little men dressed in black with small pointed caps. They are admittedly malevolent and make no bones about it. When a man dies, they scare his family with their presence, just to be hateful. They are keen on silver and gold and try to wheedle it away from the gnomes. They often carry a small shovel with them. Habitat: only in large stretches of forest, whence they undertake their raids.

goblin →
2/3 actual size

House Ghosts

This sort is very often confused with the gnome because they take on many shapes, including that of the gnome—and sometimes also of a rat, cat, or black dog. In their natural state they are invisible to man, but they can become visible in these forms. They make a lot of noise in the house at night; they live between the walls, in the attic or in the cellar, in the stable, in the shed, sometimes even in a large tree beside the house. They are not particularly intelligent, and remain friendly as long as they are treated well. They like to tease lazy people by pulling the blankets off their beds and sending icy drafts through the room. They also delight in knocking over milk pails and keeping people awake by constantly tapping on the walls.

When made very angry, they become malevolent. Their noisemaking becomes unbearable; they throw stones, the cattle become sick, drought or cold weather or continuous storms occur. They leave the house or farm only when it has been totally overwhelmed by disaster and is lost.

Trolls

Distribution area: Norway, Sweden, Finland, Russia, Siberia. Stupid, primitive, distrustful, and unbelievably ugly creatures. They have noses like cucumbers, and a tail. They are horribly strong and fast, and they stink. They often keep boxes full of stolen money and jewels, with which they play for hours, running their fingers through them.

Size: over 1 meter tall.

Hair: black and filthy.

Dwarfs

An almost extinct creature of the male sex. Height 1 meter 20 cm., often smaller. Can still be found in the middle of inhospitable forests and in the mountains. They dig for gold and silver in extensive mines, and live in groups; they are masters of metalwork. They are good-natured except for a solitary few, possibly exiles, who are capable of performing ugly deeds. If a dwarf should fall into human hands, he buys his freedom with gold. They do not have beards.

River Spirits, Wood and Mountain Nymphs

Rarefied, often invisible, beings who can take on any form; they are powerful in the magic arts. Neither good nor ill-natured as such, they avoid all trouble by simply withdrawing. But if they are pushed too far, disasters can occur. They can shed tears in a dismal fashion or laugh lugubriously; often they spy with one eye from behind a tree.

Uldras

Creatures who live underground; to be found only in Lapland. They resemble gnomes but are somewhat larger, and colorless. They live together in large families, or tribes, have authority over big wild animals such as bear, elk, wolf, and reindeer—who obey them completely. They are quite friendly, but blind as bats in the daylight. If they are mistreated by man, disasters may occur. Their ugliest method is to spread a poisonous powder over reindeer moss, causing that animal to die in large numbers and robbing the Lapp herders of their livelihood.

Relations with Other Beings

The gnome doesn't have much to do with elves, goblins, house ghosts, dwarfs, river, wood, or mountain nymphs, uldras, sorcerers, witches or werewolves, fire ghosts or fairies. He simply avoids them.

Gnomes have great difficulty with trolls, however, especially in northern Europe, Russia, and Siberia. These disturbers of the peace—meddlesome and aggressive as they are—cause endless harm to man and animals, with whom the gnome has good relations and toward whom he feels a responsibility.

Fortunately, beyond his cave the troll has no power over the gnome. Besides, the gnome is much more clever. Still, if a troll happens to catch a gnome, the most gruesome things can happen.

A favorite troll pastime is to hold the captured gnome against a revolving grindstone.

Or to hold the gnome so close to a flame that he catches fire. He is then thrown from troll to troll—the trick is to put out the flame with their sweaty hands without burning themselves!

Other atrocities: solitary confinement, a knife at the throat, or throwing a knife so that it falls within a hair's breadth of a gnome whose hands and feet are tied. Sometimes the trolls make a gnome dance attached to a chain, or put him on a treadmill—in short, anything a warped mind can think up.

The troll is not malicious enough to want to actually kill the gnome, but in spite of this the gnome sometimes becomes seriously wounded. In almost every case, however, the gnome succeeds in escaping from the troll cave, either through his own ingenuity or with outside help.

Far worse treatment awaits a gnome if he falls into the hands of a snotgurgle, of whom, mercifully, only two or three exist in the world. The snotgurgle is as large as a troll (is perhaps even related to him from primeval times), has six black-clawed fingers on each hand, enormous flat feet with seven toes on each foot. His greasy, stinking body hair is infested with lice and fleas—which seem not to bother him. Hair covers him from head to toe, even on his face, where, between greasy locks, only his gleaming, idiotic eyes can be seen.

Snotgurgles can live to be 2,000 years old, and they are born thieves. In their caves they have huge collections of gold, silver, and precious stones, which they have stolen from men throughout the years. Everything stinks of bugs.

A gnome in the power of a snotgurgle has little chance of survival. There is the case of one Olie Hamerslag (now 385 years old) who resides in the drained marshes near the Berezina. His legs were amputated by a snotgurgle who ran him through a string bean cutting machine. This gnome cunningly succeeded in escaping afterward. He was then flown home by a speckled crow, has used wooden legs for more than seventy years, and now you would hardly know it.

Alas, we also know of a gnome who lost his life: the snotgurgle put him
through a mangle. These horrible creatures have also been known to take
satanic pleasure, when they discover a gnome dwelling, in lying at the entrance
and blowing their foul, scorching breath through the house until all the gnome
furniture, irreplaceable portraits, and other cherished possessions have been
destroyed. The gnomes, of course, flee through the escape route. But they have
to begin their lives all over again elsewhere.

At present, the only snotgurgles to be found
are far beyond the Urals, and every gnome
within a thousand-kilometer radius is wise
enough to give the area a wide berth.

Snotgurgle

The Gnome and the Weather

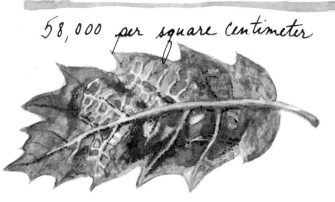

58,000 per square centimeter

Regrettably, we were unable to completely fathom the art of gnome weather forecasting. They do it with an accuracy that any professional weather forecaster would admire. When asked their secret, they mumble vaguely about "feeling it in your bones," indicate that "it just happens," or refer to "old-fashioned know-how," and so on.

We were able to learn, however, that they determine the amount of humidity in the air and the approach of low-pressure systems by the position of the stomata found on the undersides of leaves. An oak leaf has 58,000 stomata per square centimeter. The gnome, with his sharp eyes, is capable of seeing, just by looking at the leaf, if the stomata are open or shut and thus making his calculations—without the aid of computers, of course.

Gnomes also follow closely the 11-year rhythm of sunspots. A third aid comes from studying high-altitude air currents, where changes in weather first occur. This is most probably done with the help of birds.

A great joke of theirs—hoping to lead us astray, no doubt—was to show us what they called the weather tree *(Sertularia cupressina),* which droops in dry weather and revives in humid weather.

Even though the gnome knows exactly what
the weather will be long in advance, he
still goes about in rain, hail, mist, heat,
and cold — weather, after all, does not make
much difference to him.

In severe cold, however, he keeps his hands
under his beard.

As soon as even one centimeter of ice has formed on lakes, ponds, or puddles, the gnome puts on his skates. If the cold weather continues, skating races are organized.

In thunderstorms the gnome is in little danger of being struck by lightning because he is so small. If the storm really starts to rage, he takes shelter under a beech, because these trees do not attract lightning. Gnomes know the old German rhyme to ward off lightning (the hammer of Thor):

> Oak should be avoided,
> Don't stand under a willow,
> The pine is in danger,
> But beech may be safely sought.

Gnomes can forecast a windstorm unerringly, just as animals can. This knowledge is especially important to them—without it they could easily be picked up and blown away.

Snow is also accurately forecast. This is necessary because the gnome uses many openings and holes in the ground, and should these become snowed over, other arrangements would have to be made. (Mention has already been made of the long-distance skis used by gnomes after a snowstorm.)

In the mountains the gnome can predict an avalanche as surely as the chamois, fox, and deer.

The only danger that may befall gnomes in winter, especially in hilly terrain, is that if they are out walking they may get rolled up in a natural snowball as it tumbles downhill. Many a stunned gnome has been seen picking himself up out of the remains of a snowball that has splattered open against a wall or a mountain chalet.

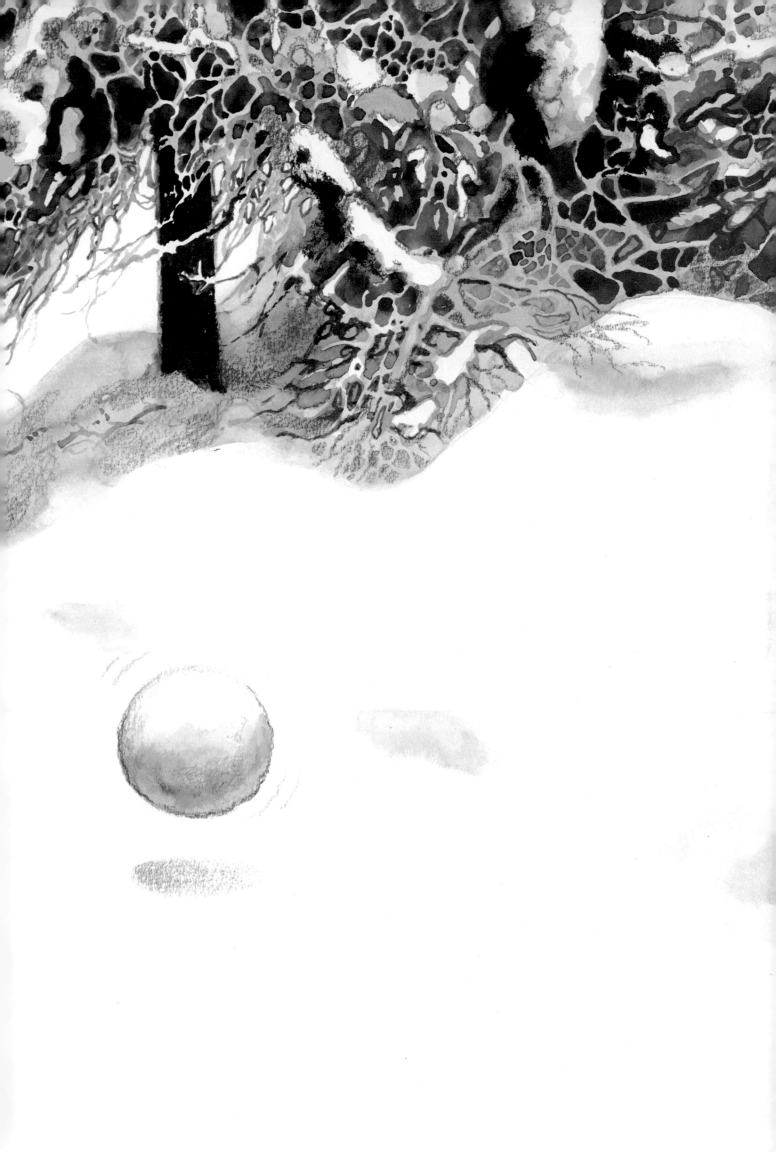

The Uses of Natural Energy

RATCHET

As simple as it is ingenious!
No noise, no smell.

← The tree, waving to and fro,
keeps the ratchet wheel in
constant motion.
Connected to the ratchet wheel
is the hammering machine with
a camshaft that rotates to
trigger the hammers. ↘

The tree is about
25 meters high,
so the pulleys are,
in reality, much smaller
↙ than shown —
about 12 mm
in diameter.

RATCHET WHEEL

CAM

RATCHET WHEEL

PEG WHEEL

FLATTENING HAMMERS
for flattening bark or crushing
oil-filled seeds.

The same method of obtaining energy
  is used for the mill.:
grinding corn or acorns,
    beechnuts, etc. —
  and for squeezing
        fruit.

RATCHET WHEEL

The Board-sawing machine

As with the hammering machine and the mill, this lumber yard device is situated in thick Blackberry bushes to prevent detection.

Indispensable for house building and gnome industry!

The handsome, smooth boards can only be produced when there is a constant breeze (see Gnome and the Weather)

Tools

double-edged handsaw

pistol-grip handsaw

the large two-man saw

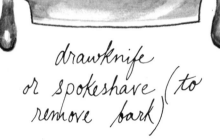

drawknife or spokeshave (to remove bark)

the sawing pit

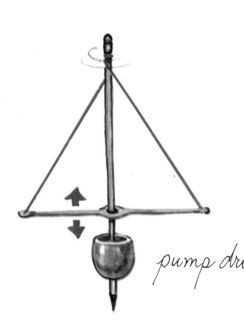

woodcarving knives

sickles

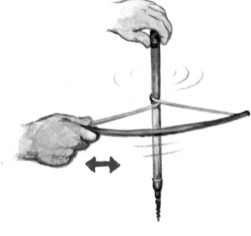

curved drill

pump drill

shears

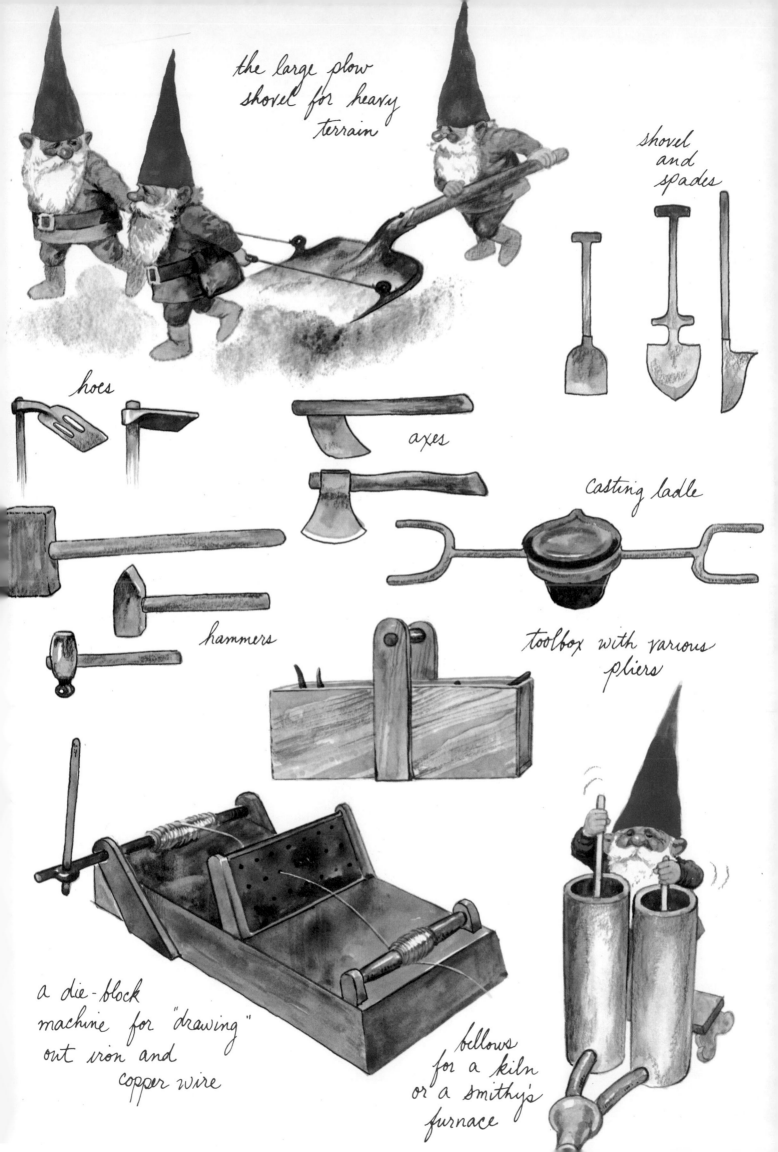

the large plow shovel for heavy terrain

shovel and spades

hoes

axes

Casting ladle

hammers

toolbox with various pliers

a die-block machine for "drawing" out iron and copper wire

bellows for a kiln or a smithy's furnace

Legends of the Gnomes

1

In a small house in the middle of a dark, sprawling forest lived a poor woodsman.

He had a wife, six children, and a black cat with one eye who kept the rats and mice at bay. The children had to walk two hours to get to school. Beside the little house was a vegetable garden and even a little flower garden; in the barn were two skinny goats and a pig.

But the family could hardly manage on the meager earnings of a woodsman, even though the father left the house before dawn and arrived home—exhausted—long after sunset. Though they had plenty of firewood and a clear stream nearby, the wife often sighed to her husband:

"How can we possibly bring up all our children?"

And the woodsman would shrug his shoulders and say he couldn't work any harder than he already did, and this was true.

One day as he was arriving home in the twilight he saw in the distance the cat leaving the woods with a rat in its mouth. But something was strange: the rat had no tail. Filled with curiosity, the woodsman approached the cat who was sitting under a bush. She hissed malevolently as he came closer, but the woodsman wasn't afraid. He grabbed the cat by the base of her tail with one hand and with the other pressed against her jaws until she opened her mouth and let the thing fall.

"Well, I'll be," said the woodsman. Because what he had picked up was not a rat, but a gnome woman. She was dead.

The woodsman had seen a gnome once, but never a female one. He took her inside and wiped away a few drops of blood on her cheeks and legs. His wife and children stroked the doll-like little being and laid her on the window seat in the living room while they ate their

meal of potatoes and bacon fat in the kitchen. When they came back, the little gnome woman was gone.

"Maybe the cat has got her again," the wife said, but the cat still sat sulking under the bush outside, showing one angry eye. The family gave up searching and went to bed, as everyone had to be up early in the morning.

The woodsman woke up in the middle of the night. Something was tugging gently at his ear. Beside his head stood a gnome. "You saved my wife," he said. "What can I do to reward you?" "But she was dead, wasn't she?" the woodsman asked, sleepily. "She was only pretending to be dead. Luckily, she's still full of life—oh, a scratch here, a few black-and-blue marks there—but she'll get over it. Just tell me what you want as a reward. Here is a little flute. When you blow on it, I'll return." And just like that—he disappeared!

The woodsman and his wife discussed the matter the rest of the night. They finally decided to ask if they might have three wishes, just as in the fairy tales.

The following evening the woodsman blew on the flute, and shortly thereafter the gnome appeared.

"I'd like to have three wishes," said the woodsman, somewhat timidly, while his wife poked at the fire behind him.

The gnome looked a little glum but finally said:

"Well, go on then—what is your first wish?"

"I want a nugget of gold so I won't have money worries anymore."

The gnome shook his head.

"You can have it, but gold seldom brings happiness."

"I don't care," said the woodsman.

"And the other two wishes?"

"We haven't decided yet."

"Well, just blow on the flute when you want me again," said the gnome with a sigh.

Next morning, there on the front steps of the little house lay a gold nugget as big as an orange, sparkling in the sun. The woodsman grabbed it up and yelled, "We're rich, we're rich!" And then he carried the nugget to the village to exchange it for money. But no one in the village had ever seen a gold nugget before and no one knew what it was worth. The blacksmith advised the woodsman to take it to a jeweler in the city. The woodsman set off at once; but instead of going the long way he took a shortcut through the swamps that he remembered from the days of his youth. As he danced along the way, admiring his gold nugget, he slipped off the path and plunged into a quagmire and immediately began to sink. He tried to reach out for firm ground, but couldn't make it. In one hand he clutched the gold nugget, and with the other he struggled to get the flute out of his pocket so that he could signal the gnome. He was barely able to reach it and blow a shrill blast.

He had sunk up to his neck in mud when the gnome appeared.

"Get me out of here," cried the woodsman.

"That is your second wish," said the gnome. He then stuck two fingers in his mouth and whistled shrilly—and in a few minutes he was surrounded by six other gnomes. Using their little axes, the gnomes chopped down a nearby tree so that it fell across the quagmire right next to the woodsman. He was able to hoist himself up onto it and get back to the path from which he had fallen. When he looked around, the gnomes had disappeared.

But still he had the gold nugget in his hand. He went on his way, muddy and shivering; eventually, his clothes dried and his courage returned. He found a jeweler in the city and entered his shop. The jeweler was a distinguished-looking man in a white smock; he wore gold-rimmed glasses. Frowning at the enormous nugget of gold and at the woodsman's bedraggled appearance, the jeweler weighed the nugget. Then he asked the woodsman to wait a few minutes and scurried out of his

shop through the back door to notify the police. A half hour later the woodsman found himself in the police station.

"And now tell us where you stole this gold," said a fat police sergeant in a fatherly fashion.

The commissioner of police asked the same question an hour later—but in a less fatherly fashion.

"I didn't steal it," cried the woodsman in despair, "I got it from a gnome."

"Of course, from a gnome," said the commissioner, who had never seen a gnome—and *would* never, because he was such an unpleasant person. "Not even one grain of gold has ever been found in this country in a thousand years—but that doesn't occur to this gentleman, does it? Lock him up!"

During the days that followed, the woodsman was questioned again and again—and threatened with dire consequences if he did not reveal the source of the gold. Finally, he was examined by a doctor, but even he could cast no light on the matter except to report that the woodsman kept babbling away about gnomes.

None of these people had ever seen a gnome because they all had ugly souls.

Meanwhile, the gold nugget was kept in the vault of the city council. After a week went by, the woodsman became so miserable that, one night, he blew the flute. After two hours, the gnome appeared.

"My wife and children are starving," the woodsman said. "I want to get out."

"That is your third wish," replied the gnome, "but I have already taken care of your wife and children." The gnome went that same night to consult a lawyer in the city who had a house gnome. Next day, the lawyer visited the police and succeeded in having the woodsman freed, owing to lack of evidence. But the gold remained behind for safekeeping until its theft could be verified.

The woodsman gladly went back to his work. The forest had never seemed so spacious and free as it did after his stay in the stuffy cell in the city; he was happy and satisfied—even though he often thought of the gold.

From that time on, things improved for him in all sorts of ways. First, a rich foreigner bought all the logs the woodsman had cut for twice the usual price. Next, the same man asked if the woodsman would become his overseer.

The happy woodsman was given a cheerful house at the edge of a village, and close to the school. He earned much more than before and his troubles were over.

A few months later he came across the gnome in the woods.

"And?" the gnome asked, "Have you got your gold back yet?"

"Not yet," the woodsman said, "It seems to be a criminal act in this country to possess gold. But even without it, my troubles are over."

"So, there you are," the gnome said—and disappeared into the bushes.

Legends of the Gnomes

2

In among the dark, warm beams of a windmill in northern Holland lived a gnome family. The miller knew them well. He had once saved the gnome wife from being crushed by the millstone. The miller always set aside milk and cornmeal for the gnome family. In exchange, they kept a watch out for fires, and warned him of coming storms or windy weather. The miller was thus always able to tie back the sails of his windmill's arms in time to prevent them from rotating wildly and possibly causing a fire due to the friction—a common hazard of windmills.

If a member of the miller's family became ill, the gnome came to call and laid his tiny, wrinkled hand on the fevered brow; he also left behind powerful medicinal herbs. This treatment usually resulted in a quick recovery.

In short, all was well in the windmill, not only physically but also financially. The miller and his wife were hardworking and intelligent and they had pleasant children.

But nearby lived some lazy folk who were less intelligent and whose wives had too free a hand with money. Envious, these vicious neighbors spread the rumor that the miller dabbled in black magic and that this was the reason for his great prosperity. Most people took no notice of these whisperings, but among the malcontents the rumors persisted.

In one of these dens of gossip lived a bright eleven-year-old girl with straw-blond braids. It was hard

to believe that she could be the daughter of such stupid and narrow-minded parents—but this sometimes happens. She knew all there was to know about animals and plants and was wonderfully gifted at modeling clay. A sweet and patient girl, one could tell that she would grow up to be a beauty. She had heard all the stories going around the village, and it became obvious to her that the miller's prosperity was due to gnomes living in the mill and not to black magic. She would have given anything to have had a gnome of her own, but because of her parents they always passed her house by.

One day at school she modeled a lifelike gnome in clay with the help of her teacher. The neighborhood potter was kind enough to fire the modeled gnome in his kiln. Afterward, the girl painted the gnome's cap blue (incorrectly, of course), his blouse red, and his pants and boots green. She also fashioned a little wooden wheelbarrow and placed the statue with it among the flowers in her parents' garden.

Her parents made fun of the statue, but they did not remove it. The gnomes in the mill heard of it, of course, and came to look at it. They were touched. As a reward they brought a present for the girl every month. And her sweetness and determination had such a good influence as the years went by that her parents became less backward and more generous. As a result—and with a certain amount of luck—they became more prosperous.

But the remaining dullards naturally misunderstood all this and muttered among themselves: "If you have a gnome statue in your garden you will become rich."

Absolute nonsense, of course. But such ideas catch on. And ever since, it has been a tradition in some homes to have a gnome—with or without a wheelbarrow—in the garden.

Legends of the Gnomes

3

The farm stood on a mound beside a seemingly endless dyke. Farther on, to the south of the river, there was nothing but vast reed- and grassland, dotted with small pools. Beyond, there was only stark loneliness, as far as the eye could see.

There were many hares, partridges, curlews, pheasants, oyster catchers, black-tailed godwits, geese, teal, swans, coots, and even otters. A gnome family lived in the roof of the farmhouse.

When winter began, the father gnome and his two 80-year-old sons warned the hares of impending high water and advised them to move. But the hares simply stared with large silly eyes, took no notice of the advice, and continued their carefree running about, chasing female hares and preening their ears.

The water began to rise at the end of February. It rained day after day, and the people living upstream were forced to build a spillway into the reed- and grassland. Cork-dry reeds and blackberry brambles were deluged overnight. The young hares were the first to drown. All

winged creatures sought safety. The adult hares were driven back onto the high ground, but as these areas too disappeared under water, the hares panicked and drowned—needlessly, for hares, like all four-footed animals, are excellent swimmers.

Finally, the plain was transformed into a large watery mirror, with here and there only a tree top, a few reed plumes, and tops of bushes to be seen. The water continued to rise.

An area of high ground not far from the dyke called the Broomstick (witches were supposed to have lived there in the old days) became the refuge for the last 8 hares to survive out of 200. But there was no shelter from the icy winds or the eyes of beasts of prey.

Water birds notified the gnomes of the hares' plight.

But the gnomes realized that they couldn't count on any human assistance because there was an unsympathetic farm worker nearby with a hunting rifle.

That evening the gnomes were fortunate enough to see the wooden gate of a picket fence floating by. The water was level with the dyke, so they lashed the gate as best they could to the land. Cleverly, they increased its buoyancy by binding loose beams and driftwood beneath it, and at about 3:00 A.M. it rose high enough out of the water to bear considerable weight.

The gnomes dragged the raft to a point where the hard northwester blew directly toward the hares' island; they jumped aboard and let the wind carry them. It was bitterly cold on the bare raft and they felt very lonely amid the dark, turbulent elements. To keep warm—and to speed up the slow-floating raft—they rowed a bit with a loose plank.

Two and a half hours later they reached the Broomstick. The hares were wet, hungry, and nervous. They ran skittishly about, stamping their hindfeet. So frightened were they that they dared not approach the raft. Whenever one would put a foot on the raft, he would pull back, run to the other side of the island, and sit huddled up and shivering.

All the while, it rained continuously and the wind sent showers of foam over animal and gnome alike.

Finally, the father gnome warned the hares in a booming voice that within two hours at most the Broomstick would be under water. They had better make haste. That got them going at last! First on board was an old mother; she was followed by the others, a tick-ridden male hare bringing up the rear.

The gnomes found it impossible to row the heavily laden raft against the wind, for in the meantime the northwester had taken on storm proportions. All they could do was to drag the raft to the other side of the island and let the wind take them. They hoped they would reach land somewhere. It was an uncertain plan, but the only one that could be carried out. The hares offered no help. They sat rolling their eyes, numbed with fear.

Fortunately, the raft proceeded with more speed than before because of the heightened storm and the eight wind-catching hare bodies on board.

The Broomstick disappeared slowly from sight. Across the water beyond the island the twinkling lights of the farmhouse, where it was safe and warm, became smaller and smaller. All around lay endless black water and curling crests of waves. The wind wailed.

The gnomes stood together and, with troubled eyes, searched a horizon that had melted into one dark mass. Everyone was soaking wet and freezing cold.

Hours later, as it began to get light, land suddenly loomed up in front of them. The raft ran aground on the edge of a new dyke road under construction. It was a wide, safe wall of sand disappearing in both directions into the lonely distance, but with lots of grass and weeds growing on it. The hares skipped off the raft, relieved, and stiffly ran away, stopping now and then to take in the new terrain with their large, frightened eyes, but never turning back with a "fare thee well" or a "thank you."

The gnomes consulted the secret maps that they had brought and planned their return route to the farm. The journey would have to be undertaken in daylight, because there was no shelter or gnome house in which to hide.

No one, however, saw the little men as they hurried forth on their long hike, not even as they crept past farms and houses—mainly because they have special techniques for this. Fortunately, too, there were still low-hanging dark clouds in the sky, and it rained at times.

By afternoon they reached home; they ate a huge meal and slept for twelve hours under the most comfortable blankets in the world.

Legends of the Gnomes

4

In Charkov, people enjoy telling this story. Just outside their village lived a certain Tatjana Kirillovna Roeslanova. She was seventy years old but still had a pretty, straight nose and shining white hair which she parted in the middle. She had been exiled from Moscow by the secret police; her husband was dead and she was without resources. Nobody was allowed to employ her, so to make a livelihood she bought a cow with money from secret friends.

Then she did something that Soviet authorities prefer not to see, but tolerate through necessity. She supplied ten houses on the outskirts of the village with milk—they would, otherwise, have had to travel so far for their milk that it would no longer be fresh when they returned. Tatjana lived in a shack in the middle of a small

vegetable garden and spent the days grazing her cow along the roadside.

There are hundreds of thousands of these one-cow businesses in Russia. The economic consequences of removing them would be so great that the government turns a blind eye.

And so Tatjana grazed her cow by day, was continually affectionate to her, and at night brought her into a corner of the shack for milking. In the opposite corner of the shack, behind a black cloth, a number of religious icons were hidden. Tatjana had managed to smuggle them from her large Moscow house, and daily she prayed before them. The cow gave 20 liters of milk a day; but there was a six-week dry period when she was expecting her calf (every year she was sent to a bull owned by a sympathetic farmer) and Tatjana had to reckon on this period in stretching her earnings over the entire year.

Although Tatjana had once been a well-to-do lady, she accepted her lot and made the best of it. She always sought out new roads, searching for the best grass for her cow, but usually returned home through the same dense alder thicket not far from her shack. In the center of the wood were a few large boulders. Under the boulders lived two gnome families with nearly adult children. Every day Tatjana stopped in the woods and picked up from under a bush a small, artfully made pitcher half the size of a jam pot. She filled it with milk from a few squeezes of the cow's udder and put it back under the bush. She did this every day, even during the scorching Russian summer heat, or biting cold, or snow, or fog and rain. And each morning following, the pitcher stood in its place again—empty and scrupulously clean.

One evening while closing the small shutters outside her shack Tatjana fell and broke her ankle. She dragged herself inside but could do nothing more. The next day she managed to milk her cow, but by evening the beast was bellowing hungrily though Tatjana had given her all the bread in the house.

The next day an ambulance stopped in front of the shack (one of Tatjana's customers had alerted the health service). A grumpy doctor examined her ankle hastily and, with the help of an attendant, rushed her off to the hospital. She pleaded with them to do something for her cow, but they shrugged their shoulders and drove on. None of her neighbors dared do anything for fear of the police.

In the hospital, Tatjana wept for her cow. Everyone she asked for help either shook their head or shrugged

Gnome milking

their shoulders. Her ankle was put in a plaster cast, and she was told that she would have to stay in the hospital for eight weeks because it was a complicated break. Tatjana worried herself sick over the cow, but soon news from home reached her.

As soon as the sun had set on the second day after Tatjana's accident, the shack door opened, the cow walked out and, without a tether, followed a gnome, who took her to the best grazing areas along the road. Just before sunrise she returned.

In the meantime, all the empty milk cans belonging to Tatjana's customers had been collected—along with the money that was left in advance to pay for the next morning's milk. In the shack, the cow was milked by the two strongest gnomes, and the filled cans were back at their respective addresses as the sun began to rise.

When Tatjana arrived home eight weeks later, with her ankle in a smaller plaster cast, she wept again, but this time from happiness and gratitude. There the cow stood,

the picture of health, and beside the ancient samovar on the wooden table lay the milk money for eight weeks and two days, neatly stacked.

When she went to bed that night, thinking about how she would be able to shuffle along the road the next day, she worried aloud that she would not be able to go very far.

"No need to," a voice behind her said. And when she turned around she saw five gnomes standing behind her humble bed.

"We've come to get the cow," the eldest said, critically looking at her plastered foot. "There is no question of your walking long distances for the time being. You go to sleep now and we'll take care of the rest. We hope you don't mind if we fill our own pitcher?"

Immediately the others ran off to gather the empty cans, and the eldest gnome, clearing his throat, took the cow on her way.

Legends of the Gnomes

5

Everyone knows that a brush fire during a long period of drought can be disastrous for man, animals, gnomes, and the countryside. What everyone is unaware of, however, is that many such fires occur that do not result in devastation.

Gamekeepers and foresters continually find places where small fires have briefly raged and in some mysterious way have been extinguished—sometimes very close to a dangerously inflammable area of brush or dry forest floor.

Just how the gnomes put out these fires is not known for certain. Sometimes, perhaps, by lighting a small counterfire (prairie Indian method); sometimes by speedily drilling into an underground stream and pumping up the water. But about other methods used we remain completely ignorant.

Legends of the Gnomes

6

The old writer sensed that his death was approaching. He lived in Norway, in a low cabin with book-lined walls in the neighborhood of Lillehammer, beside a mountain slope.

Next to the window, overlooking the valley, was a large table bearing paper, magazines, volumes of verse, inkpots, pens, candles, and more books, carelessly stacked.

One evening, just at sunset, the writer left his bed and went to sit at the table. He looked out over the peaceful valley with its lake in the distance, and recalled how he had lived here quietly for many years, and thought of how many books he had written and that soon it would all be over. Suddenly, a gnome jumped onto the table, seated himself opposite the writer, and crossed his legs. The writer greeted him happily.

"Tell me another story," he asked the aged gnome, who was holding his silver watch against his ear. "I can't think of any more, I've become too old."

"I don't know any more," the gnome said. "You've already written all the stories about this country. You've become rich from them."

"Just tell me one more. My hands are so tired, I can hardly write anymore," sighed the writer. (Nevertheless he placed pencil and notebook within reach.)

"All right then," the gnome said. He changed his position and stared outside. "Do you see that big weeping willow in the distance at the edge of the lake? The ends of its branches always hang in the water. I'll tell you why.

"Long ago, one dark night, mountain trolls switched their infant daughter with the daughter of a rich farmer, kidnapping her when everyone was asleep. Next day, the poor parents couldn't understand why their daughter's skin had suddenly become so dark or why her eyes looked like black currants. But deep in the forest the trolls exulted over the blue eyes, blond hair, and soft skin of the stolen child—and they performed a joyful, thumping dance in a circle.

"The troll child grew up to be a dark, wild tomboy and did only naughty and ugly things; she loved no one and no one loved her. One day she disappeared and was never seen again.

"But in the forest, the farmer's daughter became sweeter and lovelier every year despite all the crude and rough things she saw about her. When she was seventeen she was discovered by Olav, a strong farm laborer. (Olav slept below me in the stable of a farmhouse in the valley.) He was bringing in a few lost cows from the high mountain meadow for the winter when he saw the farmer's daughter. She was sweeping the ground in front of the troll cave under the watchful eyes of the old troll mother. It was dusk, but Olav thought he had never seen anything so fair and beautiful. He immediately fell in love. As he attempted to approach, the troll mother pulled the girl inside and locked the door.

"Back in the stable, Olav asked if I would help him,

and we set off that same night. Reaching the troll hill, we saw a stream flowing from it. (Water flows through the middle of every troll hill; they use it for drinking.) Using a divining rod, I found the spring on the other side of the hill from which the water flowed. We dug a hole, and when we reached water, Olav put me into a wooden shoe and I floated into the stuffy troll cave.

"I hid myself and the wooden shoe in a dark corner of the cave and waited until the trolls left to perform their nightly crimes in the forest. Before leaving they shut the girl in a side alcove and finally locked the main door behind them. Only the girl and I remained in the somber, stinking lair. As soon as it was safe, I released the girl and said to her: 'You're not a troll girl! Outside there's someone who will suit you much better than a troll.'

"She looked quite astonished and hesitated, but finally came along with me. Outside she saw the blond giant of a man Olav; at once she fell in love with him, as he had with her.

"The three of us ran for home. But we were still deep in the forest, and before we could make our getaway the trolls learned that we had stolen their prize. They caught up with us, beat Olav until he was black and blue, and took the girl back. I couldn't do a thing.

"A week later, we tried again. This time Olav took along a horse that he had borrowed from the farmer he worked for. For the second time, I drifted along on the underground stream into the trolls' domain. But this time

the trolls had left their old mother to stand guard. When the old mother troll turned away from a bowl of porridge she was making, I quickly tossed a good dash of sleeping potion into it. Ten minutes later she was snoring away. (I had signaled the girl not to eat the porridge.)

"Again the three of us raced through the forest for home. It was much quicker this time, on a horse. But in spite of it, the trolls caught up with us, just as we were almost out of the forest. Again they beat Olav until he was half dead, then took the girl back with them—and the horse, too, of course. There was nothing we could do; no matter how strong Olav was, the trolls were stronger.

"Three weeks later it snowed. This time I managed to get two reindeer to help us. In the trolls' cave I had to wait half the night, because not only was the troll mother on the lookout but the troll father as well! Eventually I was able to sneak enough sleeping potion into their porridge to put them fast asleep.

"The reindeer transported us quickly on a small sleigh along little-known paths in the direction of the lake. The trolls pursued us, but in the snowstorm we were lucky enough to reach the edge of the lake. I knew where an old fishing boat was moored and we got to it quickly. We cut the sleigh loose, thanked the reindeer, and sent them back to their herd. The lake was still not entirely frozen. Olav and the girl climbed aboard the boat and began rowing; I skied homeward along the bank of the lake. Nothing could happen to me. Trolls have no power over us once they

leave their cave. It was almost sunrise. The last snowflakes fell; the sky opened up and, in the east, took on a yellow and red hue.

"When the boat was already a good distance across the lake, the trolls finally reached the dock. They ranted and raved, but Olav rowed with big strokes toward the other side, and the trolls couldn't reach them. The trolls didn't have much time left: when the sun shines on them, they turn to stone. Suddenly, the strongest troll seized a gigantic boulder and hurled it at the fleeing pair. The boulder did not hit the boat, but it fell so close to it that the boat capsized. The suction dragged the girl down to the depths of the lake and she drowned. For hours, Olav dived in search of her, but he had no luck. Deeply depressed, he finally swam to the bank of the lake.

"After this, Olav was inconsolable. Every day he went to the edge of the lake and stood in one spot, staring at the water. He never looked at another girl. And when he

became so old that he couldn't work any more, he continued to return daily to the same spot. In the end, he stood there the whole day long. Branches grew out of his head and roots from his feet. And then he stood there forever. He is that weeping willow you see there at the lake's edge. Even now its branches feel about in the water in an attempt to find the drowned girl.''

The gnome looked around. The old writer had grown still. His snow-white head lay upon the notebook on the table. He was dead. The gnome smiled and went over to him. He closed the writer's eyes and read what was on the paper. The last words were, ''And then he stood there forever.''

And the gnome pulled the notebook out from under the dead writer's head, carefully loosened the pencil from his stiff fingers, and wrote the remaining sentences of the story.

Legends of the Gnomes

7

Northwest of Vastervik in Sweden, where the road divides and the great elk forest begins, stands a dilapidated church. There are a few overgrown gravestones in the small cemetery beside the church. After scraping away the moss on one of these gravestones, we can read the following text:

Here lies
SIGURD LARSSON
Born the 24th of the Hay Month 1497
Died the 30th of Summer Month 1550

Only the gnomes know that the grave under this stone contains no body.

Sigurd Larsson was a rich farmer who owned an enormous estate and grew richer year by year. He was a heavily built, unpleasant man with a cruel disposition, a coarse face, and a loud voice, which he used to shout down everything and everyone. He ruled his farm laborers ruthlessly and punished them for even the slightest offense by whipping them; milkmaids were either shut outside for the night or made to sleep in the hayloft. It was a wonder that he had any staff at all; but if anyone did leave, the influential Larsson made certain they would never find work elsewhere.

Everyone on the huge farm went silently about his work and attempted to keep out of the master's way, for he had a habit of creating false crimes just so he could punish someone. For example, he once hid some pieces of gold and then pretended to catch the so-called thief when they turned up. He often swept dirt under the carpets so that he could scold the cleaning girls. A favorite pastime of Larsson's was to hide in the summerhouse at the center of the large estate and spy on his farmhands as they worked the land. He punished them later if in his opinion they had not worked hard enough.

But his greatest satisfaction was in counting and reading IOU's. He had a cupboard full of them—all from small farmers, poor families, and neighboring villagers. It was his habit to write letters each evening in which he summoned the poor wretches to the farm to press them for payment or to plague them into signing new IOU's with an even higher interest rate.

And so life dragged by on the estate: from the outside, a gay and attractive collection of buildings on a great sweeping plain; on the inside, misery, resentment, and bitter grief. In the stables, at work, and in their sleeping places, the people mumbled curses and complaints—but only into trustworthy ears, because there were also spies about. One of those trusted was the farm gnome.

Night after night, he patiently listened to the complaints of first this one then the other, giving advice when he could. From time to time he would go to Sigurd Larsson in the evening and try to plead someone's case,

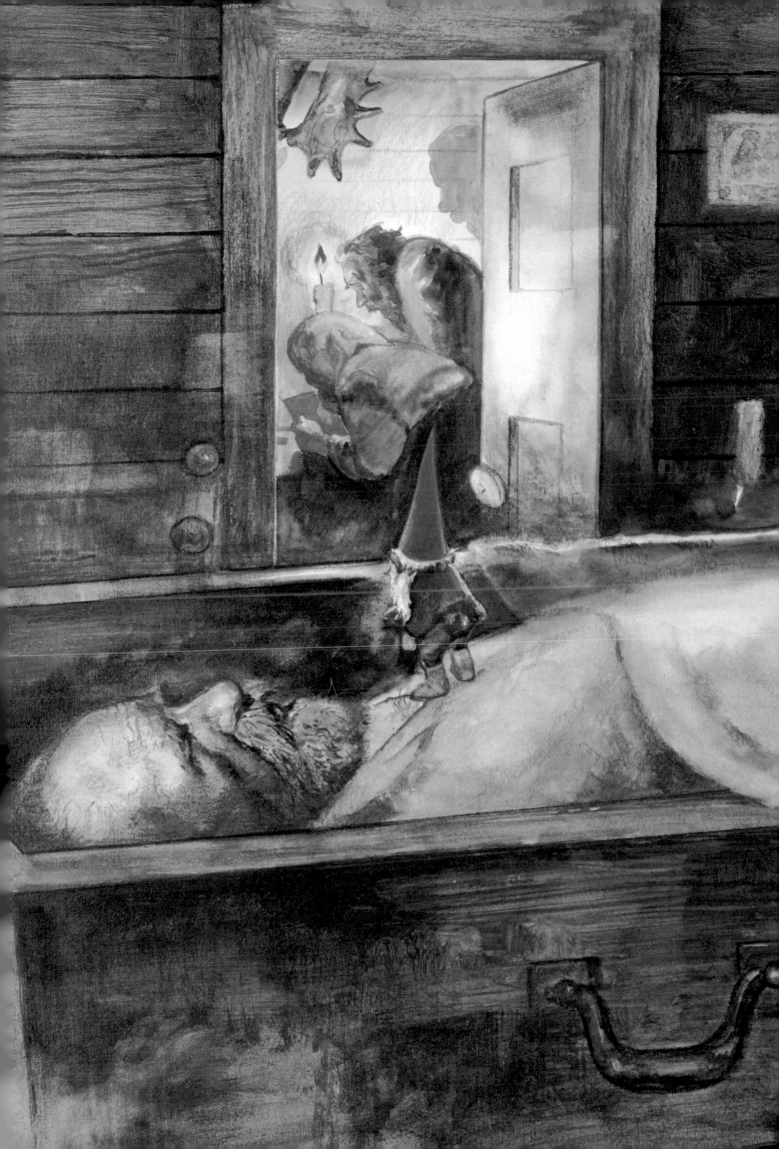

but the cruel farmer just laughed—that is, if he didn't throw an inkwell or a cup of coffee at him.

The gnome always carried himself in a very dignified way and would only say: "Just you wait, Sigurd, there'll come a time when you'll beg me for mercy on bended knee." Then the farmer would become furious and try to grab the gnome, but the gnome would always see to it that he sat in a position from which he could, with the simplest movement, escape through a chink in the wall.

Years went by. And then something began to change slowly in the big, strong body of Larsson. There were times when he felt tired, and pains shot through his arms and legs—something he'd never experienced before. At first he would just curse it away and do some cruel deed to show that he was still the same old Larsson. But his condition worsened within a few months and he began to lose weight. First a physician was sent for, then a surgeon, and then an herb doctor. None of them could diagnose his case, for all their learning, and Larsson was relieved only of a good deal of money.

After eight months, his eyes were hollow, his stomach caved in, his arms and legs were as thin as birch branches—he couldn't walk more than ten minutes without becoming tired. Finally, he went to Stockholm and Uppsala, but the professors there shook their heads, saying that there was nothing science could do to cure him.

The gnome did not let himself be seen by Sigurd for a month after his return. One evening he silently appeared when the farmer, weak and disheartened but still vicious, was going over his IOU's.

"Sigurd," the gnome said. "You're going to die."

"The farmer raised his head with a quick jerk and stared at the little man. He briefly considered throwing a book and killing the gnome, for he sat unconcerned on the edge of the table, but instead Larsson said:

"What do you know about it?"

"Everything," answered the gnome. "I even know what you need and the herb that can cure you."

And with that, he disappeared.

A week later he returned and said:

"A devil is gnawing at your nervous system and causing your muscles to dry up. They're eager to have you in hell so they can roast your black soul."

"Wait," cried the farmer, but the gnome had already disappeared. A week later he came back and said:

"I have a magic potion that can rout the devil out, but you're not going to get it." And disappeared again.

When the gnome came back during the third week, Sigurd fell on his knees and begged:

"Help me! I'll give you anything you want."

He was now just skin and bones and could hardly walk from one chair to another. But the gnome just shook his head and said:

"It will be a blessing when the world is rid of you. But first you must suffer some more."

A short time later, the insidious illness slowed the

working of Larsson's heart almost to a standstill.

And then came the morning when he did not awaken. It was the barber who found him and pronounced him dead. The priest prayed over his body, for the rest and peace of his departed soul. Everyone breathed a sigh of relief.

But the farmer wasn't dead. It only seemed that way. His heartbeat was so slow and breathing so slight that they escaped the barber's attention. But the farmer had heard everything and could just barely see through his almost closed eyelids. For the rest, he was totally paralyzed.

For a day and a half he lay in state in the death room. Servants and maids paid their respects by hissing curses at him and making faces.

On the evening before the funeral, the gnome

appeared by the coffin and said to Larsson:

"Do you hear that noise in the room next door? That is your wife and the overseer, who have broken open the cupboard. They're tearing up the IOU's."

The next day Larsson saw the light disappear as the lid was screwed onto the coffin. Then, with a deadly fear in his heart, he felt the movement of the hearse. He wanted to scream and knock on the coffin lid but he could do nothing: he was completely paralyzed. Still later, he heard dull thuds as shovelfuls of earth fell onto the coffin. And the sound of the priest's voice and the mumbling of the bystanders became more and more faint. Larsson had never known such fear. When the gravedigger finished filling in the grave, the people went home, saying, "He was nothing but a scoundrel. What luck to be rid of him."

Late that first night, eight gnomes gathered around the grave. They dug away the earth above the coffin with their shovels and pried opened the lid. The farm gnome poured a few drops from a bottle between the livid lips of the farmer. Larsson suddenly felt a wondrous power flowing through his body and opened his eyes.

"This is the healing potion," the farm gnome said. "But before we make you well you must promise never to return here. Blink three times if you agree to this."

Sigurd did so. The gnome poured a few more drops between his lips.

"You will become a woodcutter in a forest far away. Promise."

Sigurd obeyed. His heart began to beat faster and his blood began circulating. He could even lift his hand.

"You will need to use this potion for the rest of your life," the gnome said. "We will ask our brothers in the forest to provide you with it every three weeks. Don't come sneaking back here, for then you will die properly."

He then emptied the whole bottle into the farmer's mouth. Sigurd sat up shakily and then stood upright in the coffin. He could hardly believe that he was alive again. Climbing out of the grave, he breathed the cool night air. Later he could not recall if it was the fumes from the bottle or his own weakened state—but he came to his senses to find himself sitting beside a wood fire in a dark forest far from his former home. Gradually his strength returned and he lived on for another twenty years—in great poverty but happy to be alive.

Three days after Larsson's funeral an inscribed tombstone was placed above his grave. (The gnomes had filled it in again very carefully.)

At the farm there were no more beatings or nagging—on the contrary, everyone went about his work with pleasure, feeling better than ever. Larsson's wife proved to be a good mistress in whom people could place their trust. There was laughing once again on the estate, and the girls sang and danced freely at holiday time.

The summerhouse was no longer used for spying on people, but for gay Saturday night parties and long Sundays with plenty to eat and drink.

Legends of the Gnomes

8

Northern Siberia is covered by a sparse forest, half the size of Europe, called the taiga. There are also mountain chains, discovered only in 1926, in which perfectly preserved frozen mammoths have been found.

In the winter there are three hours of daylight and temperatures hover at 55 degrees below zero; amidst these bleak conditions, the northern lights offer a show of dumbfounding beauty.

Fur-bearing animals inhabit the area—the fox, small gray squirrel, lynx, mink, marten, wolf, bear, also reindeer and shaggy-haired wild ponies. Large-limbed, hardy gnomes with piercing eyes also live in the taiga; unlike woodland gnomes, they are not invariably friendly and can be vicious if crossed. These gnomes often tease the trappers who, owing to the nature of their work, spend long weeks tracking through the icy taiga. The gnomes spoil animal tracks, cause avalanches, remove trailblazing marks, imitate wild-animal calls in the night, and warn animals of the hunters' approach.

North of Oimyakon there lived a gnome named Kostja, who was much more mischievous than the rest. He was a giant of a fellow, more than half again as large as woodland gnomes—even measured in his socks. He made everyone in his part of the forest tremble with fright.

If he discovered hunters in his territory, he went to them and demanded they pay a toll: the best pelts they had. If they hesitated, he threatened to make their reindeer ill or cause them to fall off a cliff, knowing full well that the hunter depends on the reindeer for his livelihood.

Eventually all this came to the attention of the gnome king of Siberia. A stream of complaints had reached the court. Gnomes were getting a bad name, and the king decided that it was time to teach the scoundrel a lesson. So he summoned a pair of wise old gnomes; they conferred for a day and a night, and hatched a plan. Then the younger and more clever of the two was sent off to do the job.

First, the clever gnome went to the wild ponies and spoke to the leading stallion. An hour later a dozen swift ponies swarmed toward the south and formed a giant half circle. They would act as a lookout: as soon as one of them saw a hunter entering the territory of the malicious gnome he was to alert the stallion. Meanwhile the gnome galloped off to the roosting place of a friendly owl. He returned to the half circle of ponies, the owl flying alongside.

After a two-day wait the ponies signaled that a hunter, riding a reindeer, was heading in a northerly direction. The ponies were thanked and sent home, and the stallion, the owl, and the gnome followed the hunter's tracks in the snow. They waited until he had set his tent up for the night, then the gnome appeared and spoke to him. The man said he would be happy to cooperate with them in punishing the wicked gnome, as he had heard many unpleasant stories about him. Leaving the hunter with his instructions, the stallion returned the gnome to the court.

Next evening, as the hunter once more set his tent up for the night, Kostja appeared and demanded a pelt.

"Good, good," said the hunter. "Here, take my very best, a mink of excellent quality."

The gnome growled suspiciously but took the fur and disappeared with it into the forest.

Two days later, at twilight, he accidently passed the same place again and was very much surprised to see a most beautiful fox pelt hanging on a branch just over the spot where the tent had stood. The gnome remained at a distance and continued to stare silently at the pelt for a full half hour. He then circled around it three times, peering at it suspiciously; finally, he decided that it was all right. The hunter must have forgotten it. A windfall.

In his greed, Kostja did not see the owl, pressed tightly against the trunk of a spruce tree a short distance away, and he began to climb the tree to retrieve the fox pelt. It had a smooth trunk with few branches, and the gnome had to use his hands and feet in order to get a firm grip. When the gnome was halfway up, the owl suddenly swooped down and snatched the cap from his head. The gnome ranted and raved so much that he lost his grip and fell to the ground with a thud. Too late: the owl, with the cap in his claws, was flying high above the trees toward the palace.

The icy night was far from agreeable to the bareheaded gnome. The only thing he could do was to pull the collar of his jacket over his freezing head and hurry home. He was so angry that he stayed indoors for a week (giving his poor wife a terrible time). Now, he could have made a new cap by making felt from some of the furs in the house, but a cap is an irreplaceable possession for a gnome; he wanted his own back, no matter what the consequences.

Although he was wicked, this gnome was far from stupid. He knew that there was more to the matter than met the eye. Even so, it was ten days before he could summon up the courage to cover his head with two of his

wife's kerchiefs and present himself to the king. He had lost weight and felt humiliated.

At court he was coolly received and had to wait three hours before the king and his council granted him an audience. The king sat on a dais. He was smaller than the gnome but he radiated an air of absolute authority. There, at the king's feet, lay the cap.

"I hope that this has taught you a lesson, Kostja," he said. "None of us are angels, but your behavior has left much to be desired. You may have your cap back if you give away all your furs to the first hunter you see. Do you understand?"

"Yes," mumbled the guilty gnome.

The king placed a foot under the cap and flipped it
into his arms, saying: ''Put it on outside. You may go.''
   The giant gnome felt very small. He turned around,
went out the door, left the palace, and did what he had
promised, for gnomes, be they good or bad, always keep
their word.

It was the end of January. A severe northeasterly wind was blowing and the thermometer registered 30 degrees below zero. Everything in the fields and woods was frozen stiff, and the gnomes' outdoor activities were reduced to a minimum, unless, of course, someone was in need of help.

In the cozy, safe houses under the trees, games were played and stories told. Imp Rogerson thought up something new every night. His great-grandfather had known Wartje, the magic goldsmith who dared to do everything, and had told stories about him to his son, who had told them to his son, who told them to Imp.

One night, Imp's twin daughters, tired and sleepy-eyed from playing, sat at their father's feet and begged for a new story about Wartje.

"Have I told you how Wartje got back the gold and precious stones a dragon had stolen and returned them to the elves of Thaja?"

"Yes."

"And how, to save the life of a little human girl who lay dying, he plucked a life-giving herb from an island in Siberia that was guarded by a ferocious dinosaur?"

"Yes."

"And how, during a storm, he slipped off the back of an osprey and fell into the middle of the bewitched lake of Warnas, and was brought to shore by a blind carp?"

"Yes."

"And how he was captured by the trolls?"

"No."

"All right then. Wartje was always falling out with trolls. As he was far too clever, they couldn't stand him. You remember that Wartje had three houses—one in Poland, one in the Ardennes, and one in Norway—so that he could carry out his many tasks. In Norway he always had problems with jealous trolls. Now, Wartje rode a large fox who ran more swiftly than the wind. He could travel from one house to another, even with his wife and goldsmithing tools aboard, in less than one night.

"Once when Wartje was in Norway, the trolls dug a

hole alongside a path he normally used. Wartje and his fox
passed that way a few nights later. They had been on a
long, tiring journey and were both extremely hungry.

"As they neared the trap, the fox smelled a strong
odor of mouse and dashed into the hole. (The trolls had
crushed a number of mice with their filthy fingers and
smeared them on the sides of the hole.) Before Wartje and

his fox realized it, they were trapped. Wartje must have been very tired to have been tricked in such a fashion. But they could do nothing. The trolls took them through an underground passage into their cave and shut Wartje behind bars in a side alcove. The fox was put in chains.

" 'Now you will forge gold for us,' the trolls said to Wartje. 'We'll never set you free.'

"Every day they pushed a nugget of gold through the bars and ordered:

" 'Make a bracelet, a ring, a necklace. You won't get a mouthful of food until they are finished.'

"And they threw an old bone to the fox, that is, if he was lucky enough not to get a well-placed kick instead. Wartje had to follow their orders because he had found no way to escape, and he had to think of the plight of the poor fox as well.

"The trolls wore the bracelets, rings, and necklaces on their misshapen arms, necks, and sausage-like fingers. They danced and danced in their filthy cave until the sweat ran off their bodies and the place stank worse than usual.

"When, after two weeks, Wartje had not returned, his wife, Lisa, began to worry. Wartje had often stayed away in the past, but never as long as this. One night she went out to search for him, which was very brave of her. She asked all the animals she met if they had heard anything of her husband, but none of them had. At last, at the foot of the mountains Lisa ran into a rat who had fled

the troll cave where Wartje was held captive, because the stench was too much even for him.

"'You'll never get him out,' the rat said, 'They'll only catch you as well. I can tell you that they keep the key to the side alcove in the third crack in the wall beside the fireplace. On the main door there is only one bolt, but it is too high for you to reach.'

"That evening, Lisa made a plan. She gathered together some pans, rotten eggs, beans, and devil's dung (asafetida), a gum resin that trolls adore but can never get because the plant which produces it grows in faraway Persia. They love it because of its horrible smell.

"Lisa disguised herself as a sorceress with a tall pointed cap covering her own cap and a black robe, set up a wood fire on a flat rock not far from the troll cave, and began to cook her brew. Before long the revolting smell was wafted into the cave and the trolls, following their noses, waddled curiously outside.

"'What's going on here?' they asked suspiciously, a bit afraid of the little sorceress.

"'Nothing exceptional, noble sirs,' Lisa replied. 'I am a poor sorceress and am preparing my simple evening meal.'

"'Hummm,' growled the trolls enviously. 'It smells good.'

"'Would you like to taste some?' Lisa asked. 'But only a mouthful for each, as this is all I have.'

"The trolls tasted a mouthful and declared that they had never tasted anything so delicious.

"'I see you enjoy this simple food,' Lisa said. 'It happens that I will be here tomorrow. Do return, with your entire family. How many people should I count on?'

"'Five,' the trolls said, more dim-witted than usual because they could think of nothing but the heavenly taste on their tongues.

"'Good. Come just before sunset, then. You can let your own fire go out because I will prepare enough food to last for three days. I won't be here myself, as I have business in the neighborhood.'

"The next evening the trolls found five portions of

Gnome Music

Every gnome dowry chest has inside it a music box which begins to play when the chest is opened. These music boxes are highly prized and are made from wood of the best quality, with the finest spring-steel mechanisms. In most homes the music-box tune is based on the heroic poem about the legendary Swedish gnome Thym, who lived between 1300 and 1700.

the Troll Pimple

wood!

the girl from Uppsala

the legendary gnome Thym

The Song of the Troll

1. Old   Pimple is a   fearsome troll with   louse-filled hair,   so I am told.
4. (When) Pimple grabbed, his   hand b'came wood, Thym   left the for-est   feel-ing good.

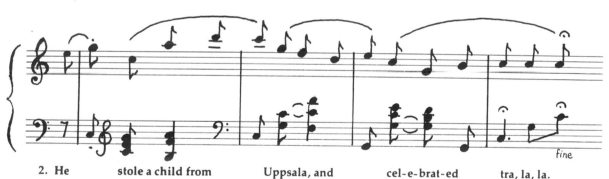

2. He   stole a child from   Uppsala, and   cel-e-brat-ed   tra, la, la.
5. He   took the child to   Uppsala, and   cel-e-brat-ed   tra, la, la.

3. Then   good gnome Thym came   on the scene, put   devil's glue where   gold had been.   When

2.

When a gnome goes to the toilet he doesn't lock the door: a music box plays, indicating that the room is in use. The action is triggered by a secret handle upon entering the room. The words of the tune played are not sung, but are well known. In many gnome houses, the text of the song hangs beside the toilet door, and the tune is often hummed by members of the family as they wait.

While the music box plays, the gnome spends his time usefully. In this room, over the years, many artistic objects are made— such as carved portraits, toys, and attractively fashioned household utensils.

Do Not Disturb

The mu-sic plays when we use this room; a gnome law ho-nored from of old;

And while the tune un- folds its notes, I do not wish to be dis-turbed.

So while you wait con- tain yourself, and keep a cool head and warm feet;

Let noth-ing you dis- turb at all, the while you sigh so pa-tient-ly,

But settle down con- tent-ed-ly while drinking dande- li-on tea.

A Conversation with Tomte Haroldson

Eventually we were working on the last chapters, the required number of pages having been filled. One of the gnomes we often talked to during our research for this book was the now 379-year-old Tomte Haroldson. He lives in the flax fields near Amersfoort, in Holland.

One cold evening at about midnight, Tomte came unexpectedly, which he had never done before. All the doors and windows were closed against the inclement weather, but this had not hindered him.

He greeted us calmly, acted friendly but distracted, as always, and seated himself on the studio table. He apparently knew that our work was almost done and had come to satisfy his curiosity, which pleased us no end. We cheerfully gave him an acorn cup of fruit wine and a cashew nut cut into three pieces. He took a sip, turned the cup around pensively in his fingers, looked about him, and asked:

"How is it coming along?"

"Beautifully," we cried. "We're almost finished."

"And exactly as you wanted it?"

"Well, it can always be improved," we said modestly (not believing it).

"Then you think it is all right as it is?"

"Of course, why not?"

"May I see how it has turned out?"

We placed a thick pile of sketches and text in front of him and let him see everything, from the beginning. He looked at page after page without saying a word, now and then stopping us when he wanted to study a sketch or a sentence more thoroughly, and thoughtfully munched on his cashew. His silence bothered us so much that we looked at each other glumly from time to time.

He was through at 1:30 A.M. He hadn't opened his mouth since the first page, except when he wanted to chew on a nut. Our uncertainty increased. A deathly silence reigned.

Tomte raised his acorn cup and we quickly refilled it. He peered into the depths of the fruit wine, sniffed at it, then pointed at the pile of pages and asked: "Is that the whole book?"

"Well, no, not all of it," we quickly replied. "We still have to add and change a few things here and there, but all in all, we think we've covered just about everything."

He looked at us one at a time. His gaze was deep and penetrating, as if a distant land lay behind his eyes (gnomes often have this quality).

"Am I to understand that the life and deeds of my people, for the first time in history, have been completely recorded in this?"

"Well, yes . . . more or less," we said. The little man radiated an air of remarkable authority, even though he remained seated all the while (yet another quality gnomes often possess).

Tomte nodded, and downed his drink in one swallow.

"So, this is all we have to tell you," he said, staring dreamily out the window into the darkness. "I had hoped for more."

"What do you mean 'more'? What more is there?" we asked, nervously. Our high spirits had long ago left us. Tomte didn't seem too happy either.

He pressed his hands between his knees and said, without looking up at us, "It is all very charming—delightful sketches, good stories. But something has been omitted, something has not been acknowledged. And it would be too much for us gnomes to bear if this something were left out of a book like this. Just a minute, I want to show you something." He suddenly jumped down to the floor, ran away, then came back a few minutes later carrying a leather-bound book.

"My Family Book," he said casually. "I had it hidden outside."

He sat on the table again, put on his glasses, and turned to the middle of the book.

"We don't write down only family affairs," he said, winking his eye. "If you use that magnifying glass, you can read along. I have written it in your language."

He became serious again and indicated a date at the top of one of the pages. "I'll take just a few examples. First point: population distribution. Do you recognize this date?"

We nodded silently. It was the year we had begun our gnome studies, thinking that we were observing them without their knowing. Tomte turned to a map of one of our Dutch provinces which covered two pages. On this map, all of our camouflaged observation huts and hideaways were clearly marked and numbered.

He looked at us over the top of his glasses.

"Or were there more?"

"No."

It was a long time ago but we remembered it just as if it had been yesterday.

"Look," he said, "here it is. That year, we were spied upon three hundred and twelve times."

We were dumbfounded.

"And you thought we weren't on to you? Dear friends, you could never, with those big feet, stomp about someone's private world without being noticed. We even heard you giggling."

He turned some more pages, but it wasn't necessary. We hadn't captured them; they had captured us. It was embarrassing.

"All right," we said, defeated. "That was in the beginning. And you let us see only what you wanted us to see. But later weren't we allowed to look about freely?"

Tomte laughed a bit shyly.

"That's why I'm here tonight. Now we come to the second point: the disappointment. We were on to you and knew those aspects of our lives you were focusing on—our cleverness, our cuteness, our technical innovations, our humor. That couldn't do any harm; besides, you meant well, and that's why we went along with it. If they're so bent on portraying our outer shell, we said to one another, we'll just play along with them. Then maybe later they'll have brains enough to dig deeper."

We began to understand what he meant. Indeed, we had mainly paid attention to superficialities. He laughed again.

"But it couldn't go on that way or, rather, end that way. You both had become too dear to us for us to allow that. And that's why I'm here tonight. Sent here, I might add."

A long silence followed. It began to dawn on us that we, through our self-complacency, had only scratched the surface in our gnome studies.

"It seemed a shame to us that you might send the book to the publisher without our first having had a talk. For now we come to point three: balances. Let me begin this way. All of us come from the universe and the earth—indeed, you people say it yourselves: 'Of dust man was made, and to dust will he return!' Of course, we'll all return to the universe and the earth. But we have remained true to our origins, while you haven't. Our relation with the earth rests on harmony, yours rests on abuse—abuse of living and dead matter."

"Not everyone does this," we protested.

"Fortunately not. But mankind as a whole leaves behind it a trail of destruction and exploitation."

"Don't gnomes ever upset nature's balance?"

"No. Man runs wildly about in the world of today and lives almost always at nature's expense. The gnome has found peace in the world of yesterday and is satisfied with what it has to offer. There won't be any change in this, just as there won't be any change in salmon, who for thousands of years have swum from the middle of the ocean to the rivers of their birth . . . just as the bee who finds good pollen does a dance to call the other bees . . . or as the pigeon finds its destination thousands of kilometers away. . . ."

"That has to do with instinct. Aren't we digressing a bit?"

"Not at all. Now we come to point four: *we* have our instinct and intellect in proper balance; you have subordinated your instinct to your intellect."

"But we are only human. Our minds take over . . . that's the way we are made. Instinct doesn't offer enough security."

"It offers insufficient security only if you imprison it under a glass bell. Give me a little more wine."

"But human beings long for the restoration of nature, as she was in her old glory."

"And that's why we must proceed in three ways: the restoration of instinct, the restoration of balance in nature, and less striving for power."

"Why are you throwing that in?"

"Because all the other evils on earth stem from the craving for power. You know that just as well as I do."

"Don't you gnomes ever struggle for power?"

"No. We have tossed all power politics overboard."

"That is of course much easier to do in a gnome society, where you have no population problem."

"Overpopulation is something you must be able to overcome among yourselves; we have already done so."

"Is this all included in the perfect harmony that the gnomes have achieved?"

"Yes."

Here we had reached an impasse in our discussion. No doubt their world is harmonious and stable, but one might also think their world monotonous. Even so, imagine meeting a stag with colossal antlers on a lonely path beside the woods, as gnomes can and do. No one would want to miss something like that.

Tomte walked back and forth on the table, his hands clasped behind his back. "Fifth point: You must not think that we despise man's civilization—though nature has had to pay dearly for it—or that we can't appreciate its good points. But there is an immense gap between what you understand as progress and what we understand as progress. When we see the idiotic and ugly things you do, we can only shake our heads in wonder. I have collected a few examples of these."

He picked the book up once again, turned a few more pages but suddenly slammed it shut while he slipped his eyeglasses into the bag attached to his belt.

"It is too late now," he said. "I have a few things to do before sunrise."

"Tomorrow night at 10:30," Tomte said. He pointed at us cheerfully. "Look at you both, just sitting there. Surely you're not going to let yourselves become discouraged?"

He tapped on the manuscript.

"It will be a magnificent book. Or otherwise we can always do something about it. You can please me by adding a chapter; call it Why Gnomes Shake Their Heads.' "

And he disappeared.

Why Gnomes Shake Their Heads

Although a great gap lies between your idea of progress and ours," Tomte said the following evening, seated in a doll's armchair, the book on his knee, "we do follow yours from a distance. Take the example of Rembrandt van Rijn. My brother Olie knew him very well. Olie lived under an old lime tree near Rembrandt's house beside a canal in Amsterdam, and he spent countless evenings in a dark corner drawing alongside the master.

"Many times he shook his head in wonder at the stupidity and narrow-mindedness of the men who commissioned the paintings, the abuses Rembrandt suffered, and the awful poverty he endured at the end of his life. He saw the famous *Nightwatch* progressing stroke by stroke, a masterpiece now admired almost to distraction. Shaking his head and with pain in his heart, he saw how the painting was sawed down to make it small enough to fit through the door, when it was later moved to the Town Hall after Rembrandt's death.

"And what did you humans do with the good doctor Semmelweis in 1865? Do you suppose we didn't hear about it? What we had known for hundreds of years was finally discovered by man: that the delivery of an infant must be carried out with clean hands so that neither the child nor the mother will become infected. Semmelweis was simply hounded to death by his opponents."

Tomte pushed his glasses onto his forehead and looked at us.

"That is what I meant last night."

"Well, yes, but we also know this. Throughout history the most incredible stupidities have occurred. We too shake our heads at this."

Tomte lowered his glasses again and turned some more pages.

"The difficulty seems to be that humans simply do not recognize a great man in his lifetime, especially if he is an artist."

"That is because some artists create works for which the people are not yet prepared—except for a small devoted circle. Only after one or two generations does recognition come."

"In the meantime the artist has died, forgotten. Think about one of your most famous composers. I have it firsthand from Timme Friedel. Timme is a small, dreamy gnome who left Vienna in despair in 1791 and now lives in a rock dwelling in the countryside. Now, we gnomes may not have a Mozart among us, but we would surely have offered a man of such talents a more dignified way of leaving this world.

"The conversations between Mozart and Timme are written in a small book that your historians would give their eyeteeth to get hold of. Timme always knew how to help Mozart out of a somber mood. He had only to ask Mozart to give him a violin lesson to make the master laugh like a child. He would then spend hours giving Timme his lesson.

"So it was with tears in his eyes that the devoted Timme, defying daylight, snow, and rain—followed Mozart's poor funeral procession (which cost 11 florins and 56 kreuzer) on 6 December 1791. Everyone left the procession at the churchyard gate, owing to the bad weather. Timme was the only living soul who stayed on. Shaking his head he saw how the gravedigger literally threw the coffin into a pauper's grave and then hurried off to find shelter.''

Tomte shut the book but kept his finger between the pages.

''We just can't understand it,'' he said.

He turned to the following page.

''What you have done to plants and animals is also beyond description. That the elk, brown bear, and wolf have disappeared from these parts does have something to do with changes in climate, I will admit, but the extermination of the beaver was inexcusable. The last beaver was shot in 1827 at Zalk beside the Zuider Zee and we thus lost forever a dearly loved friend with whom we had had the most cordial relations and who had provided us voluntarily with a very special type of fat. And if you, with your traffic and poisons, murder the last remaining specimens of green frog, prudent toad, and yellow-bellied fire toad, it won't be simply a matter of a few more animal species disappearing.

''No. Profound disturbances in the natural balance of things will make years of extra work for us. This is not to mention the harm done to us personally by your poisons. I will decline to comment on the miserable state of birds of prey or their infertile eggs. You humans have become nature's enemies.

''Look here: of the 1,300 plant species, 700 are in danger; the succulent leaf is almost extinct. I won't even mention the salmon, sturgeon, or shad—all river fish that have locally disappeared. Three-fourths of your people don't even know they ever existed. You can, of course, pretend to be lords and masters of creation, but that is no reason to carry on like beasts—though a beast would behave less callously."

"Look, we two are in complete agreement with you."

"I know, I know. Can't I grumble just a little? Do you know another sickening habit? I believe people leaving on vacation, as you call it, are responsible. They throw cats and dogs out of their cars, abandoning them in the woods. You should see the poor wretches. They grieve and starve in a miserable manner. One or two survive and become poachers, and then nobody is safe."

We shrugged and said:

"They are scoundrels, indeed, who should never be allowed to keep pets. But there is, alas, little to be done about it."

He nodded and picked up the book. He flipped through the remaining pages.

"There is much more in here about the destruction of our good and beautiful world, but let's stop now, otherwise it will become monotonous. Just this, though, because it so disturbs us: stop making war. In my lifetime alone there have not been twenty-five years without a war going on somewhere in the world.

"Well, that's that. I've had my say. Now we three are going to take a walk; I want to reward you both for your many years of toil."

Outside, the full moon had risen a hand's breadth above the horizon. The tree tops stood out starkly against the cloudless sky. The night was deathly still, except for the faint rattling of a train in the distance. It was mild, and spring hung in the air.

We entered a path heading southwest. Although we were both very familiar with the area, after about five minutes we no longer knew where we were. But Tomte led the way with a sure stride and we followed.

Had we been walking for an hour? Two hours? Twenty-four hours? We couldn't for the world remember. It appeared not to be a planned walk but a predestined wandering.

Time stood still and nature embraced and enclosed us like a warm sea. We were weightless; we were ageless; we knew everything that had been forgotten. Tomte had endowed us with gnome qualities for this night.

We met a fox. He stood still, sniffed at us inquisitively with no sign of fear. A pregnant doe allowed us to scratch her between the ears and stroke her thick winter coat. A hare proudly showed us her first litter of the year. Rabbits continued their games in our presence. We spoke to wild boars and a marten.

We were questioned by an owl. We watched two endlessly playful badgers. We heard the trees breathing, bushes whispering, the mumbling of moss; we listened to secret tales of centuries past; we melted into every living cell on earth, recognized every dimension, and our souls were in equilibrium and peace.

As the moon began to pale, we completed an

unfathomable journey through an unknown dimension.

Tomte raised his hand. We stood still as he continued on up a hill.

"This is the way nature can be if you remain true to her. I wish you all the best. *Slitzweitz.*"

He walked on alone up the hill. Our hearts were sad. Beside an old pine tree he turned, raised his hand once more—this time in farewell—shook his head softly but with a smile on his small face, and disappeared over the hill.

Everything fell away like old music that is suddenly interrupted. We were ordinary mortals once again. Dawn was breaking, the sun would soon rise. At that moment we saw where we were. In the flax fields, no more than half an hour away from home.